Collins

SCHOOL WORLD ATLAS

Contents

COLLINS SCHOOL WORLD ATLAS
Collins
An imprint of HarperCollins Publishers
Westerhill Road, Bishopbriggs, Glasgow G64 2QT

© HarperCollins Publishers 2013
Maps © Collins Bartholomew Ltd 2013

First published as Foundation World Atlas 2005, reprinted 2007
First published as Collins School Atlas 2008, reprinted 2008
Second Edition 2010, reprinted 2010, 2011 (twice)
Third Edition 2013, reprinted with changes 2014, 2015

ISBN 978 0 00 748441 6

Imp 003

The contents of this edition of the Collins School World Atlas are believed correct at the time of printing. Nevertheless the publishers can accept no responsibility for errors or omissions, changes in the detail given, or for any expense or loss thereby caused.

British Library Cataloguing in Publication Data
A catalogue record for this book is available from the British Library.

Printed and bound in Hong Kong

All mapping in this atlas is generated from Collins Bartholomew digital databases. Collins Bartholomew, the UK's leading independent geographical information supplier, can provide a digital, custom, and premium mapping service to a variety of markets. For further information:
Tel: +44 (0) 208 307 4515
e-mail: collinsbartholomew@harpercollins.co.uk

Visit our websites at:
www.collins.co.uk
www.collinsbartholomew.com

The Solar System

The Solar System is the Sun and the many objects that orbit it. These objects include eight planets, at least five dwarf planets and countless asteroids, meteoroids and comets. Orbiting some of the planets and dwarf planets are over 160 moons. The Sun keeps its surrounding objects in its orbit by its pull of gravity which has an influence for many millions of kilometres.

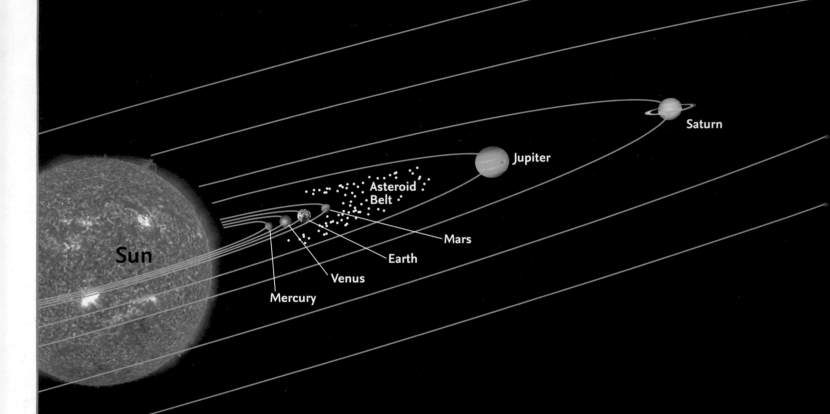

Sun

Mercury
Venus
Earth
Mars
Asteroid Belt
Jupiter
Saturn

The Sun

Diameter
1 391 016 km
Circumference
4 370 000 km
Average temperature
5504 °C
Rotation about axis
(measured at its equator)
25 Earth days 9 hours

The Planets

	Mercury	Venus	Earth	Mars
Diameter	4900 km	12 100 km	12 700 km	6779 km
Circumference	15 300 km	38 000 km	40 000 km	21 300 km
Distance from Sun	58 million km	108 million km	150 million km	228 million km
Length of year	88 Earth days	244 Earth days 17 hours	365 days 6 hours	687 Earth days
Length of day	59 Earth days	243 Earth days	23 hours 56 minutes	24 hours 37 minute

	Jupiter	Saturn	Uranus	Neptune
Diameter	143 000 km	116 500 km	50 700 km	49 200 km
Circumference	450 000 km	366 000 km	159 000 km	154 700 km
Distance from Sun	778 million km	1427 million km	2871 million km	4498 million km
Length of year	11 Earth years 314 days	29 Earth years	84 Earth years	165 Earth years
Length of day	9 hours 55 minutes	10 hours 39 minutes	17 hours 14 minutes	16 hours 7 minute

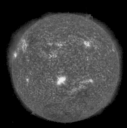

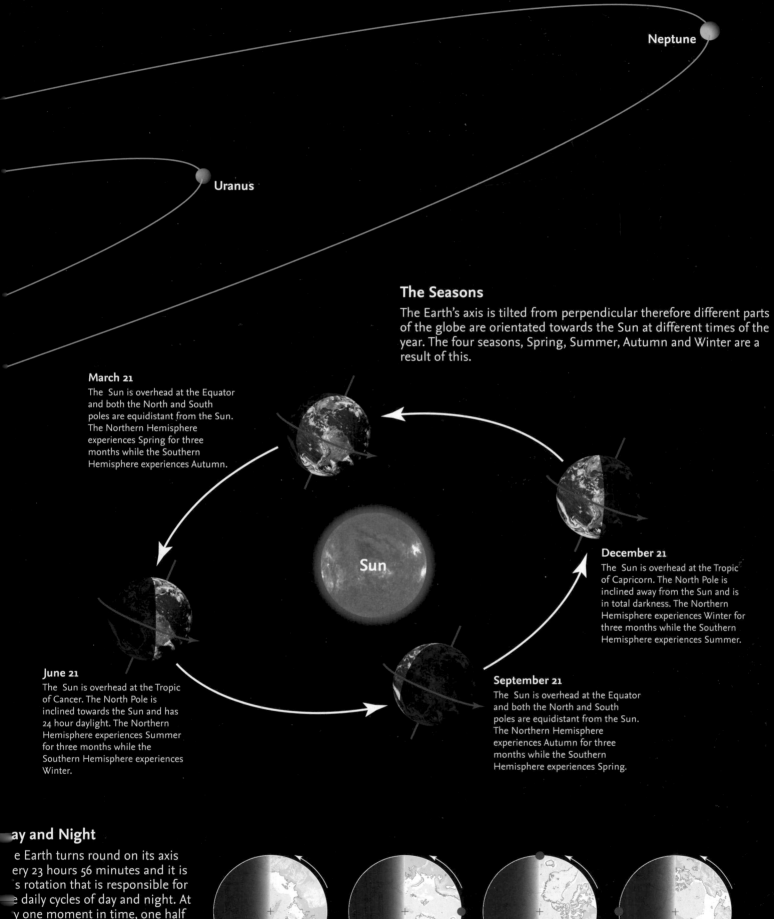

Neptune

Uranus

The Seasons

The Earth's axis is tilted from perpendicular therefore different parts of the globe are orientated towards the Sun at different times of the year. The four seasons, Spring, Summer, Autumn and Winter are a result of this.

March 21
The Sun is overhead at the Equator and both the North and South poles are equidistant from the Sun. The Northern Hemisphere experiences Spring for three months while the Southern Hemisphere experiences Autumn.

December 21
The Sun is overhead at the Tropic of Capricorn. The North Pole is inclined away from the Sun and is in total darkness. The Northern Hemisphere experiences Winter for three months while the Southern Hemisphere experiences Summer.

June 21
The Sun is overhead at the Tropic of Cancer. The North Pole is inclined towards the Sun and has 24 hour daylight. The Northern Hemisphere experiences Summer for three months while the Southern Hemisphere experiences Winter.

September 21
The Sun is overhead at the Equator and both the North and South poles are equidistant from the Sun. The Northern Hemisphere experiences Autumn for three months while the Southern Hemisphere experiences Spring.

Sun

ay and Night

e Earth turns round on its axis
ery 23 hours 56 minutes and it is
s rotation that is responsible for
e daily cycles of day and night. At
y one moment in time, one half
the Earth is in sunlight, while the
her half, facing away from the
n, is in darkness. As the Earth
ates it also creates the apparent
ovement of the Sun from East to
est across the sky.

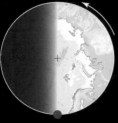

Dawn

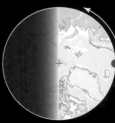

Midday

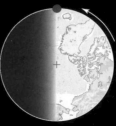

Dusk

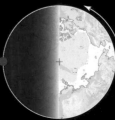

Midnight

A Political Map

Map A uses different colours to show clearly the shape of each country. A line is used to represent the international boundary around each country. It is possible to see the relative areas of the countries. Capital cities and other major cities are shown by symbols on a Political map.

B Rainfall Map

The colours on Map B represent areas which have the same range of annual rainfall. From this type of map it is possible to find the wettest or driest region in a country. Rainfall maps are often accompanied by climate graphs such as the one shown at the bottom of the opposite page.

Using Atlas Maps

An atlas includes different kinds of maps and diagrams. The different parts of an atlas page are shown on the map below which is a reduced version of page 32 in the atlas. In order to understand maps it is important to understand the labels and information which appear on each page. The example below is a reference map which

Using Atlas Maps

1. **Page Title**
   The page title explains what area or topic the map covers.

2. **Page Number**
   The page number is essential when using the index or contents page.

3. **Letters and Numbers**
   These form a grid which make it easy to find places listed in the index eg Naples is in grid square F4.

4. **Lines of Latitude**
   These show how far north or south of the Equator a place is located.

5. **Facts Box**
   Information in the Facts Box is subdivided into various categories. An icon (or symbol) identifies each of the categories which are explained below.

Facts Box

The information listed in the **Facts about...** box is explained below.

Landscape: Indicates the area and highest point.

Population: Lists the total population and the average number of people living in one square kilometre.

Settlement: Shows the percentage of the population living in cities and towns. The main towns and cities are also listed.

Land Use: Main crops grown and the main industries in the region are identified here.

Development Indicators: Four indicators are shown here.

Life expectancy: The number of years a newborn child can expect to survive.

GNI per capita: The annual value of production of goods and services of a country, per person.

Primary school enrolment: The total of all ages enrolled at primary level as a percentage of primary age children.

Access to safe water: Percentage of the population with reasonable access to sufficient safe water.

shows a variety of information such as settlement, communications, the physical landscape and political borders. In this atlas there are also many thematic maps which give information on one or two special topics. Maps A, B, C and D to the left and right of the reference map are typical examples of four different types of thematic map.

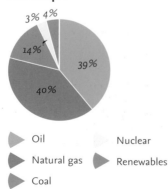

Facts about Italy

Landscape
Area: 301 245 sq km
Highest point: Mont Blanc 4810 m

Population
Total: 60 789 000
Density: 202 persons per sq km

Settlement
% Urban population: 68
Main towns: Rome, Milan, Naples, Turin

Land use
Main crops: Sugar beets, corn, grapes
Main industries: Machinery, metal products, chemicals, food

Development indicators
Life expectancy: male 79, female 84
GNI per capita: US$ 35 330
Primary school enrolment ratio: 97
% Access to safe water: 100

11 Lambert Conformal Conic projection

Using Atlas Maps

6 Locator Map
The locator map shows the position of the map in a wider region.

7 Key Box
Every map has a key which explains the symbols used on the map. The use of symbols on the maps in this atlas are explained in more detail on page 8.

8 Scale Bar and Ratio Scale

9 Lines of Longitude
These show how far east or west of the Greenwich Meridian a place is located.

10 Compass
The compass shows the direction of north, south, east and west. Maps are usually drawn with north at the top of the page.

11 Projection Note

C Relief Map

Map C shows the height of the land. Areas which are the same height above sea level are shown in the same colour. Lowland is shown in green and the highest mountain areas in brown or purple. The landscape features are named on a relief map and symbols are used to show the main mountain peaks. From this map we can see that Kilimanjaro is the highest peak in Africa.

D Population Map

The colours used on this map show the distribution of the population in the rural areas. Different sizes of dot show the distribution of cities and towns. Together the different colours and different size dots show where most of the people of Kenya live.

Graphs

Information in this atlas is often presented as a graph or diagram. Three examples of graphs used are shown to the right.

Pie graphs are circles divided into segments to show percentage values.

Bar graphs can be used to compare quantities between different topics or countries.

Climate graphs are a combination of bars and lines.

Pie Graph

3% 4%
14%
39%
40%

◀ Oil   ◀ Nuclear
◀ Natural gas ◀ Renewables
◀ Coal

Bar Graph

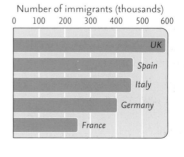

Number of immigrants (thousands)
0   100   200   300   400   500   600

UK
Spain
Italy
Germany
France

Climate Graph

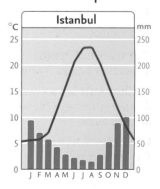

Istanbul

°C   mm
25   250
20   200
15   150
10   100
5   50
0   0
   J F M A M J J A S O N D

Latitude and Longitude

Lines of latitude are imaginary lines which run in an east-west direction around the globe. They run parallel to each other and are measured in degrees, written as °. The most important line of latitude is the **Equator**, 0°. All other lines of latitude have a value between 0° and 90° North or South of the Equator. 90° north is the North Pole and, 90° south, the South Pole.

Lines of longitude are imaginary lines which run in a north-south direction between the **North Pole** and the **South Pole.** The most important line of longitude is 0°, the **Greenwich Meridian**, which runs through the Greenwich Observatory in London. Exactly opposite the Greenwich Meridian on the other side of the world, is the 180° line of longitude. All other lines of longitude are measured in degrees east or west of 0°.

When both lines of latitude and longitude are drawn on a map they form a grid. It is easy to find a place on the map if the latitude and longitude values are known. The point of intersection of the line of latitude and the line of longitude locates the place exactly.

The Equator can be used to divide the globe into two halves. Land north of the Equator is the **Northern Hemisphere.** Land south of the Equator is the **Southern Hemisphere.** The 0° and 180° lines of longitude can also be used to divide the globe into two halves, the **Western** and **Eastern Hemispheres.** Together, the Equator and 0° and 180°, divide the world into four areas, for example, North America is in the Northern Hemisphere and the Western Hemisphere.

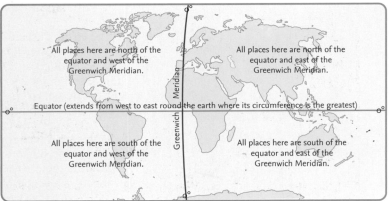

Using Scale

The **scale** of each map in this atlas is shown in two ways:

1 The **Ratio scale** is written, for example, as 1 : 1 000 000. This means that one unit of measurement on the map represents 1 000 000 of the same unit on the ground.

eg **Scale 1 : 1 000 000**

2 The **line** or **bar scale** shows the scale as a line with the distance on the ground marked at intervals along the line.

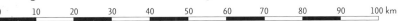

Different Scales

The three maps to the right cover the same area of the page but are at different scales. Map A is a large scale map which shows a small area in detail. Map C is a small scale map which means it shows a larger area in the same space as Map A, however in much less detail. The area of Map A is highlighted on maps B and C. As the scale ratio increases the map becomes smaller.

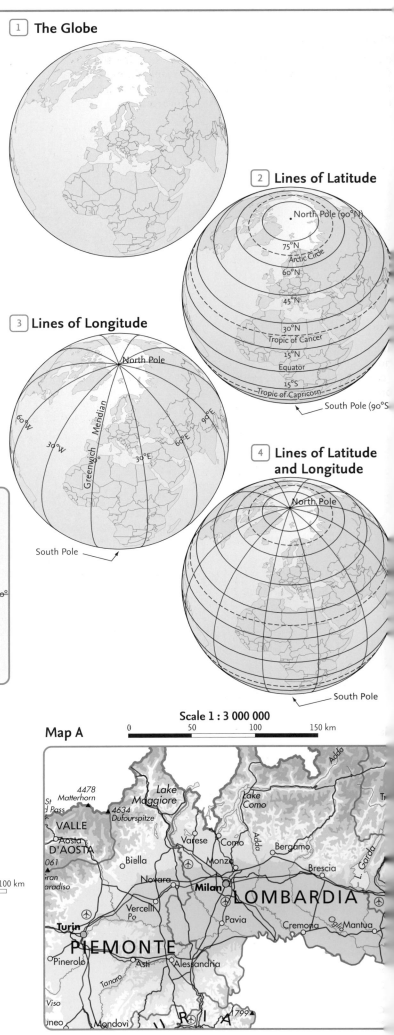

1 **The Globe**

2 **Lines of Latitude**

3 **Lines of Longitude**

4 **Lines of Latitude and Longitude**

Scale 1 : 3 000 000

Map A

Mapping the world

To show the world on a flat map we need to peel the surface of the globe and flatten it out. There are many different methods of altering the shape of the earth so that it can be mapped on an atlas page. These methods are called **projections**.

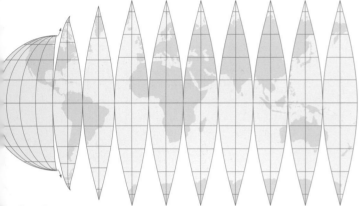

Projections

Map projections change the shape and size of the continents and oceans. The projection used for world maps in this atlas is called Eckert IV. How the world map looks, depends on which continents are at the centre of the map.

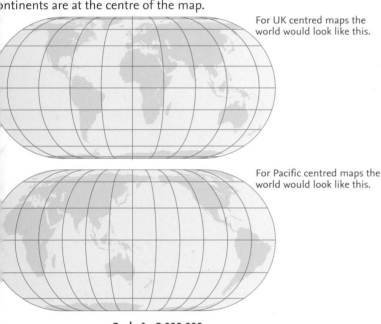

For UK centred maps the world would look like this.

For Pacific centred maps the world would look like this.

Measuring Distance

The scale of a map can also be used to work out how far it is between two places. In the example below, the straight line distance between Brasília and Salvador on the map of Brazil is 7 cm. The scale of the map is 1 : 15 000 000. Therefore 7 cm on the map represents 7 X 15 000 000 cm or 105 000 000 cm on the ground. Converted to kilometres this is 1050 km. The real distance between Brasília and Salvador is therefore 1050 km on the ground.

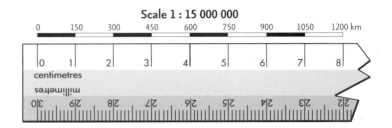

Scale 1 : 15 000 000

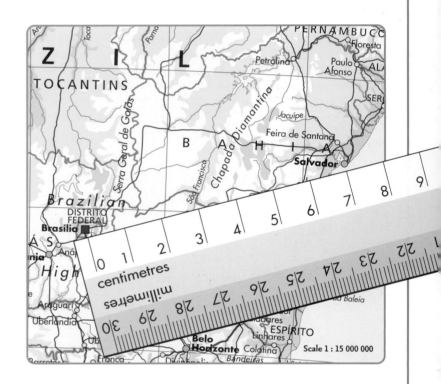

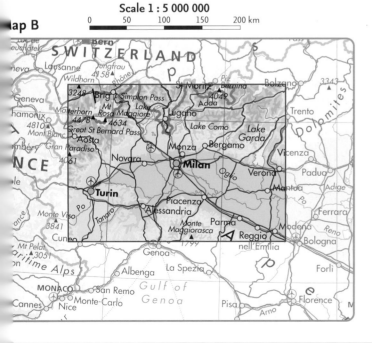

Scale 1 : 5 000 000

Map B

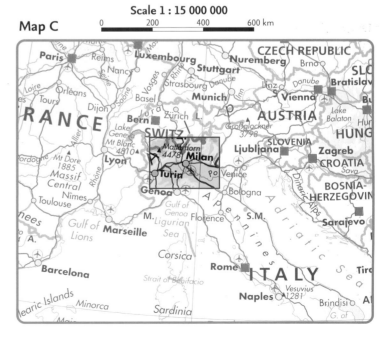

Scale 1 : 15 000 000

Map C

Symbols

Maps use **symbols** to show the location of a feature and to give information about that feature. The symbols used on each map in this atlas are explained in the **key** to each map.

Symbols used on maps can be dots, diagrams, lines or area colours. They vary in colour, size and shape. The numbered captions to the map below help explain some of the symbols used on the maps in this atlas.

Different styles of type are also used to show differences between features, for example, country names are shown in large bold capitals, small water features, rivers and lakes in small italics.

Using Grids

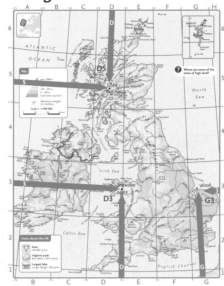

The map on the left shows the British Isles. Lines of latitude and longitude are numbered in 2° intervals in the map frame. These form a **grid** on the map. Large letters and numbers, together known as **alphanumerics,** are used to label the horizontal and vertical columns made by the grid.

The alphanumerics can be used to identify the **grid square** in which a feature is located, for example

> Ben Nevis is in D5,
> Snowdon in D3,
> The Wash in G3.

1	⌇	**River** The largest and most important rivers are shown.
2	✈	**Airport** Main international airports are shown.
3	●	**Large City** This symbol is used to show cities with over 500 000 people.
4	■	**Capital City** All capital cities, large or small are shown with the same symbol.
5	⌇	**Railway** **Road** Railways and roads are the main links between the towns and cities.
6	⬭	**Lake** Lakes and areas of water are shown in a pale blue tint.
7	○	**Other Town or City** Cities or towns with less than 500 000 people are shown as a small yellow dot.
8	⌇	**International Boundary** International boundaries mark the edges between one country and another. They give a country a distinctive shape by which we can often identify it.

A. ANDORRA
L. LIECHTENSTEIN
LUX. LUXEMBOURG
M. MONACO
MON. MONTENEGRO
NETH. NETHERLANDS
S.M. SAN MARINO

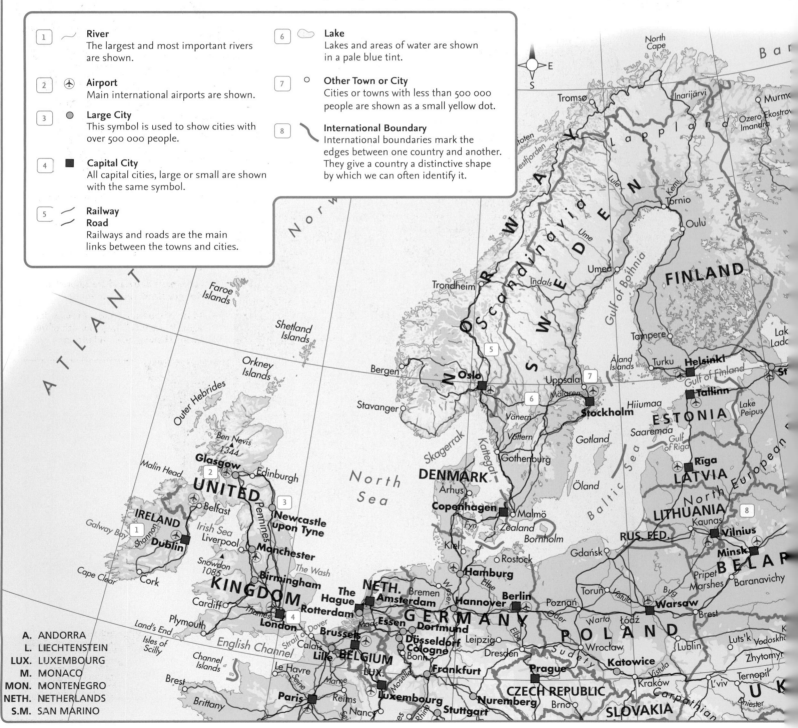

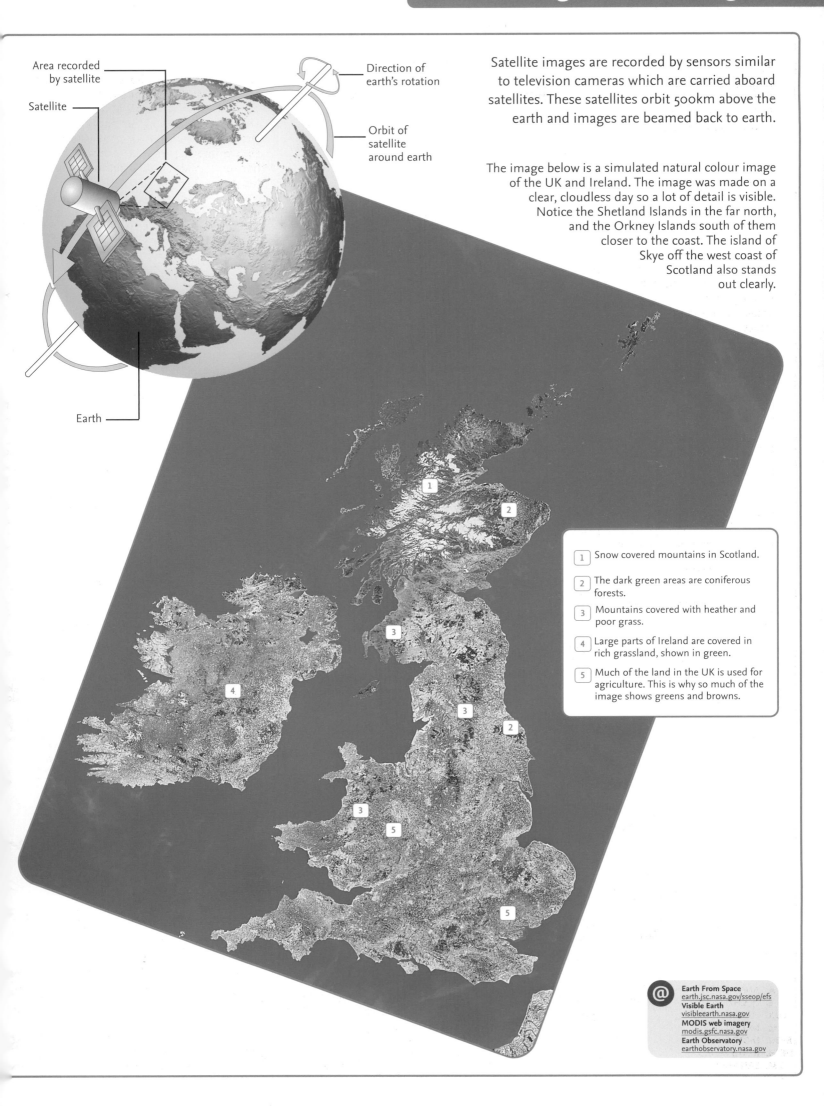

Area recorded by satellite

Satellite

Direction of earth's rotation

Orbit of satellite around earth

Earth

Satellite images are recorded by sensors similar to television cameras which are carried aboard satellites. These satellites orbit 500km above the earth and images are beamed back to earth.

The image below is a simulated natural colour image of the UK and Ireland. The image was made on a clear, cloudless day so a lot of detail is visible. Notice the Shetland Islands in the far north, and the Orkney Islands south of them closer to the coast. The island of Skye off the west coast of Scotland also stands out clearly.

1 Snow covered mountains in Scotland.

2 The dark green areas are coniferous forests.

3 Mountains covered with heather and poor grass.

4 Large parts of Ireland are covered in rich grassland, shown in green.

5 Much of the land in the UK is used for agriculture. This is why so much of the image shows greens and browns.

@ **Earth From Space**
earth.jsc.nasa.gov/sseop/efs
Visible Earth
visibleearth.nasa.gov
MODIS web imagery
modis.gsfc.nasa.gov
Earth Observatory
earthobservatory.nasa.gov

What is GIS?

GIS stands for **Geographic Information System.** A GIS is a set of tools which can be used to collect, store, retrieve, modify and display spatial data. Spatial data can come from a variety of sources including existing maps, satellite imagery, aerial photographs or data collected from GPS (Global Positioning System) surveys.

GIS links this information to its real world location and can display this in a series of layers which you can then choose to turn off and on or to combine. GIS is often associated with maps, however there are 3 ways in which a GIS can be applied to work with spatial information, and together they form an intelligent GIS:

> **1. The Database View** – the geographic database (or Geodatabase is a structured database which stores and describes the geographic information.

> **2. The Map View** – a set of maps can be used to view data in different ways using a variety of symbols and layers as shown on the illustration on the right.

> **3. The Model View** – A GIS is a set of tools that create new geographic datasets from existing datasets. These tools take information from existing datasets, apply rules and write results into new datasets.

Why use GIS?

A GIS can be used in many ways to help people and businesses solve problems, find patterns, make decisions or to plan for future developments. A map in a GIS can let you find places which contain some specific information and the results can then be displayed on a map to provide a clear simple view of the data.

For example you might want to find out the number of houses which are located on a flood plain in an area prone to flooding. This can be calculated and displayed using a GIS and the results can then be used for future planning or emergency provision in the case of a flood.

A company could use a GIS to view data such as population figures, income and transport in a city centre to plan where to locate a new business or where to target sales. Mapping change is also possible within a GIS. By mapping where and how things move over a period of time, you can gain insight into how they behave. For example, a meteorologist might study the paths of hurricanes to predict where and when they might occur in the future.

GIS USERS

The National Health Service	Environmental Agencies
The Police	Councils
Estate Agents	Supermarkets
Government Agencies	Insurance Companies
Schools	Banks
Emergency Services	Holiday Companies
The Military	Mapping Agencies

GIS Layers

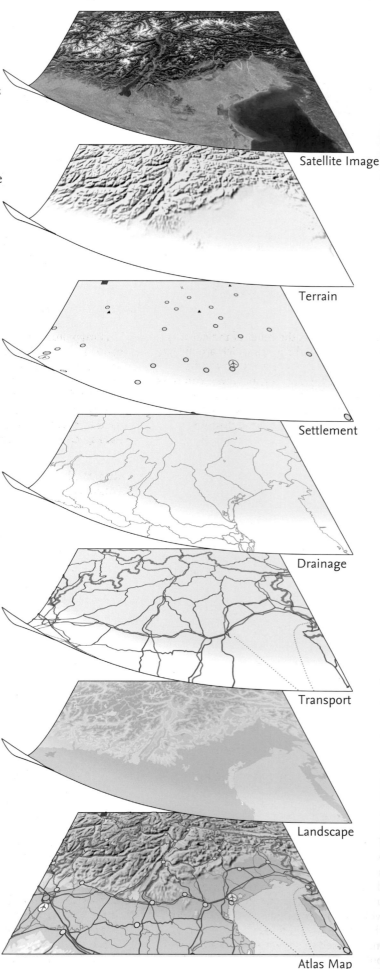

Satellite Image

Terrain

Settlement

Drainage

Transport

Landscape

Atlas Map

Terrain

This map shows the relief of the country, and highlights the areas which are hilly in contrast to flatter areas. Relief can be represented in a variety of ways - contours and area colours can both show the topography. This terrain map uses shading which makes the hilly areas obvious.

Energy Sources

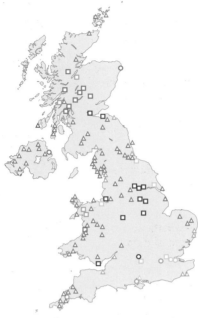

This map illustrates the location of energy sources in the UK using point symbols. Each point symbol contains coordinate information and represents the different types of energy sources, for example the blue triangles show the location of wind farms. Points can be used to represent a variety of features such as banks, schools or shopping centres.

Transportation

Roads shown here have been split into two categories, Motorways in green and Primary Roads in red, and these have been attributed with their road number. This is a road network using linear symbols. Rivers and railways could also be shown like this.

Land Use

This Land Use map illustrates the different ways in which the land is used in areas across the UK. Each area is coloured differently depending on the type of land use. Areas in yellow are dominated by farms which grow crops, whereas urban areas are shown in red and forests in green. This map is used to show agricultural land use, but a similar map could be used to show different types of soils for example.

Regional Migration

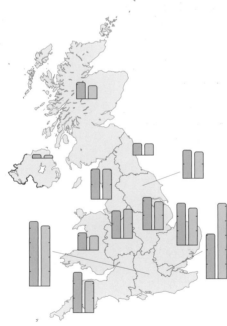

Graphs can be used on maps as a type of point symbol, and are an effective way of representing changes over time. This map has been divided into the regions of Britain and shows the number of people moving in and out of each region. The orange bar shows the number of people (in thousands) moving into an area, and the green bar shows the number of people moving out.

Population Distribution

Population distribution can be shown on a map by using different colours for each category. This map uses 3 categories and each shows the number of people in a square kilometre. The yellow areas contain less than 10 people per square km; the light orange areas have 10 – 150, whilst the dark orange areas contain over 150 people per square km. The dark orange areas therefore have the highest population density.

United Kingdom

SCOTLAND

WALES ENGLAND

Edinburgh

London

Cardiff

Belfast

NORTHERN IRELAND

IRELAND

Facts about the United Kingdom

Landscape
Area: 244 082 sq km
Highest point: Ben Nevis 1344 m

Population
Total: 62 417 000
Density: 256 persons per sq km

Settlement
% Urban population: 80
Main towns: London, Birmingham, Manchester, Leeds, Glasgow

Land use
Main crops: Wheat, barley
Main industries: Food products, machinery, transport equipment, chemicals

Development indicators
Life expectancy: male 79, female 82
GNI per capita: US$ 37 780
Primary school enrolment ratio: 100
% Access to safe water: 100

Key

	International boundary
	National boundary
	Administrative boundary
■	Capital city
○	Administrative centre

Scale 1 : 3 000 000

0 25 50 75 100 km

N
W E
S

SHETLAND ISLANDS
Lerwick

ORKNEY ISLANDS
Kirkwall

WESTERN ISLES
(NA H-EILEANAN SIAR)
Stornoway

HIGHLAND
Inverness

MORAY
Elgin

ABERDEEN-SHIRE

ABERDEEN CITY
Aberdeen

S C O T L A N D

ARGYLL AND BUTE
Lochgilphead

PERTH AND KINROSS
Perth

STIRLING
Stirling

ANGUS
Forfar

DUNDEE CITY
Dundee

FIFE
Glenrothes

EAST LOTHIAN
Haddington

Edinburgh
Dalkeith
MIDLOTHIAN
Livingston

SCOTTISH BORDERS
Newtown
St Boswells

SOUTH LANARKSHIRE
Hamilton
Motherwell

NORTH AYRSHIRE
Irvine
Kilmarnock
EAST AYRSHIRE
Ayr
SOUTH AYRSHIRE

RENFREW-SHIRE
Paisley
Greenock
Dumbarton
Glasgow

NORTHUMBERLAND
Morpeth
NORTH TYNESIDE

Ballycastle
MOYLE
Coleraine
COLERAINE
Limavady
Ballymoney

SCOTLAND
1. INVERCLYDE
2. WEST DUNBARTONSHIRE
3. EAST RENFREWSHIRE
4. GLASGOW CITY
5. EAST DUNBARTONSHIRE
6. NORTH LANARKSHIRE
7. FALKIRK
8. CLACKMANNANSHIRE
9. WEST LOTHIAN
10. EDINBURGH

NORTHERN IRELAND
1. NEWTOWNABBEY
2. CARRICKFERGUS
3. BELFAST
4. CASTLEREAGH
5. NORTH DOWN

? **What are the sub-regions of the UK?**

Boroughs of Greater London

Barking and Dagenham
Barnet
Bexley
Brent
Bromley
Camden
City of London
Croydon
Ealing
Enfield
Greenwich
Hackney
Hammersmith and Fulham
Haringey
Harrow
Havering
Hillingdon
Hounslow
Islington
Kensington and Chelsea
Kingston upon Thames (admin. centre for Surrey)
Lambeth
Lewisham
Merton
Newham
Redbridge
Richmond upon Thames
Southwark
Sutton
Tower Hamlets
Waltham Forest
Wandsworth
Westminster

Merseyside and Greater Manchester

ROCHDALE
Rochdale
OLDHAM
Oldham
BURY
Bury
Bolton
BOLTON
WIGAN
Wigan
SALFORD
Salford
MANCHESTER
Manchester
Ashton-under-Lyne
TAMESIDE
Stockport
STOCKPORT
Stretford
TRAFFORD
Southport
SEFTON
ST. HELENS
St Helens
KNOWSLEY
Huyton
Bootle
Wallasey
LIVERPOOL
Liverpool
WIRRAL

East Berkshire

SLOUGH
Slough
Maidenhead
WINDSOR & MAIDENHEAD
Bracknell
BRACKNELL FOREST
Reading
READING
Wokingham
WOKINGHAM

WALES

1. BLAENAU GWENT
2. MERTHYR TYDFIL
3. TORFAEN
4. CAERPHILLY

IRELAND

ENGLAND

WALES

FRANCE

BELGIUM

CUMBRIA
NORTH YORKSHIRE
EAST RIDING OF YORKSHIRE
CITY OF KINGSTON UPON HULL
NORTH LINCOLNSHIRE
NORTH EAST LINCOLNSHIRE
LANCASHIRE
WEST YORKSHIRE
SOUTH YORKSHIRE
LINCOLNSHIRE
DERBYSHIRE
NOTTINGHAMSHIRE
CHESHIRE
STAFFORDSHIRE
LEICESTERSHIRE
RUTLAND
SHROPSHIRE
WEST MIDLANDS
WARWICKSHIRE
NORTHAMPTONSHIRE
NORFOLK
SUFFOLK
CAMBRIDGESHIRE
BEDFORD
CENTRAL BEDFORDSHIRE
HEREFORDSHIRE
WORCESTERSHIRE
MONMOUTHSHIRE
GLOUCESTERSHIRE
OXFORDSHIRE
BUCKINGHAMSHIRE
HERTFORDSHIRE
ESSEX
GREATER LONDON
KENT
EAST SUSSEX
WEST SUSSEX
SURREY
WILTSHIRE
SWINDON
WEST BERKSHIRE
HAMPSHIRE
ISLE OF WIGHT
SOMERSET
DORSET
DEVON
CORNWALL
ISLE OF ANGLESEY
GWYNEDD
CONWY
DENBIGHSHIRE
FLINTSHIRE
WREXHAM
POWYS
CEREDIGION
PEMBROKESHIRE
CARMARTHENSHIRE
NEATH PORT TALBOT
SWANSEA
BRIDGEND
RHONDDA CYNON TAFF
VALE OF GLAMORGAN
CARDIFF
NEWPORT
ISLE OF MAN
CHANNEL ISLANDS (UK)
Guernsey
Jersey
Alderney
ISLES OF SCILLY

NORTHERN IRELAND
OMAGH
FERMANAGH
DUNGANNON AND SOUTH TYRONE
ARMAGH
NEWRY AND MOURNE
DOWN
ARDS
CRAIGAVON
BANBRIDGE

UK National Statistics
www.statistics.gov.uk
The Scottish Parliament
www.scottish.parliament.uk
Northern Ireland Office
www.nio.gov.uk
The National Assembly for Wales
www.assemblywales.org

Conic Equidistant projection

ATLANTIC

OCEAN

over 1000m
500 – 1000 m
200 – 500 m
100 – 200 m
0 – 100 m
land below sea level

1344 ▲ Mountain height (in metres)

Scale 1 : 4 000 000

? **Where are some of the areas of high land?**

Facts about the UK

◆ **Area**
244 082 sq km

︿ **Highest peak**
Ben Nevis, 1344 metres

▱ **Largest lake**
Lough Neagh, 396 sq km

North

Sea

Shetland Islands
Unst
Yell
Fetlar
Foula
Mainland
Bressay
Sumburgh Head
Fair Isle

Fair Isle

Westray
Sanday
Orkney Islands
Stronsay
Mainland
Hoy
Pentland Firth
South Ronaldsay
Duncansby Head

Cape Wrath
Thurso

Butt of Lewis
Isle of Lewis
Clisham
799
Harris
Outer Hebrides
St Kilda

North Uist
South Uist
Barra

The Minch

Loch Shin
Dornoch Firth

North West Highlands

Skye
Cuillin Hills
993

Rum

Coll
Tiree
Mull
Ben More
966

Inner Hebrides

Firth of Lorn
Jura
Islay

Loch Ness
Spey
Deveron
Cairngorm Mts
Ben Macdui
1309
Dee
Don
Rattray Head
Moray Firth

Ben Nevis
1344
Grampian Mountains

Ben Lawers
1214
Loch Tay
Tay
Loch Awe
Loch Lomond
Forth
Ochil Hills
Firth of Tay
Firth of Forth

St Abb's Head
Clyde
Ayr
Tweed
Holy Island
Southern Uplands
Cheviot Hills

Arran
Firth of Clyde
Mull of Kintyre
Clyde

Merrick
843
Nith

Malin Head
Errigal
752
Foyle

Donegal Bay
Lower Lough Erne
Bann
Antrim Hills
Lough Neagh
Lagan

Upper Lough Erne
Mourne Mts
Slieve Donard
852
Dundalk Bay

North Channel

Mull of Galloway
Solway Firth
St Bees Head
Scafell Pike
977
Lake District
Eden
Tees
The Pennines
Wharfe
Ouse
North York Moors
Derwent
Flamborough Head

Erris Head
Achill Island
Lough Conn
Lough Mask
Lough Corrib
Galway Bay
Aran Islands

Shannon
Suck
Lough Ree
Lough Derg
Shannon

Boyne
Liffey
Barrow
Nore
Suir

Wicklow Mts
Wicklow Head

Isle of Man
Calf of Man
Morecambe Bay
Ribble

Irish
Sea

Anglesey
Mersey
High Peak
Trent
Spurn Head
Mouth of the Humber

Caernarfon Bay
Snowdon
1085
Dee
Witham
The Wash

Cardigan Bay
Cambrian Mountains
Severn
The Fens
Wensum
Norfolk Broads
Little Ouse
Waveney

Teifi
Wye
Severn
Avon
Great Ouse
Cam
Chelmer

St George's Channel
St David's Head

886
Brecon Beacons
Cotswold Hills
Thames
Chiltern Hills
Thames

Carmarthen Bay
Worms Head
Avon
Mendip Hills
Salisbury Plain
Avon
Test
North Downs
Leith Hill
294

Dingle B.
Carrantuohill
1041
Blackwater
Lee

Bristol Channel
Lundy
Hartland Point
Exmoor
New Forest
South Downs
Dungeness
Beachy Head

Celtic Sea

Exe
Yes Tor
619
Dartmoor
Lyme Bay
Stour
The Solent
Isle of Wight

Bodmin Moor
Tamar
Bill of Portland

Cape Clear
Land's End
Lizard Point
Isles of Scilly

English Channel

Lambert Azimuthal Equal Area project

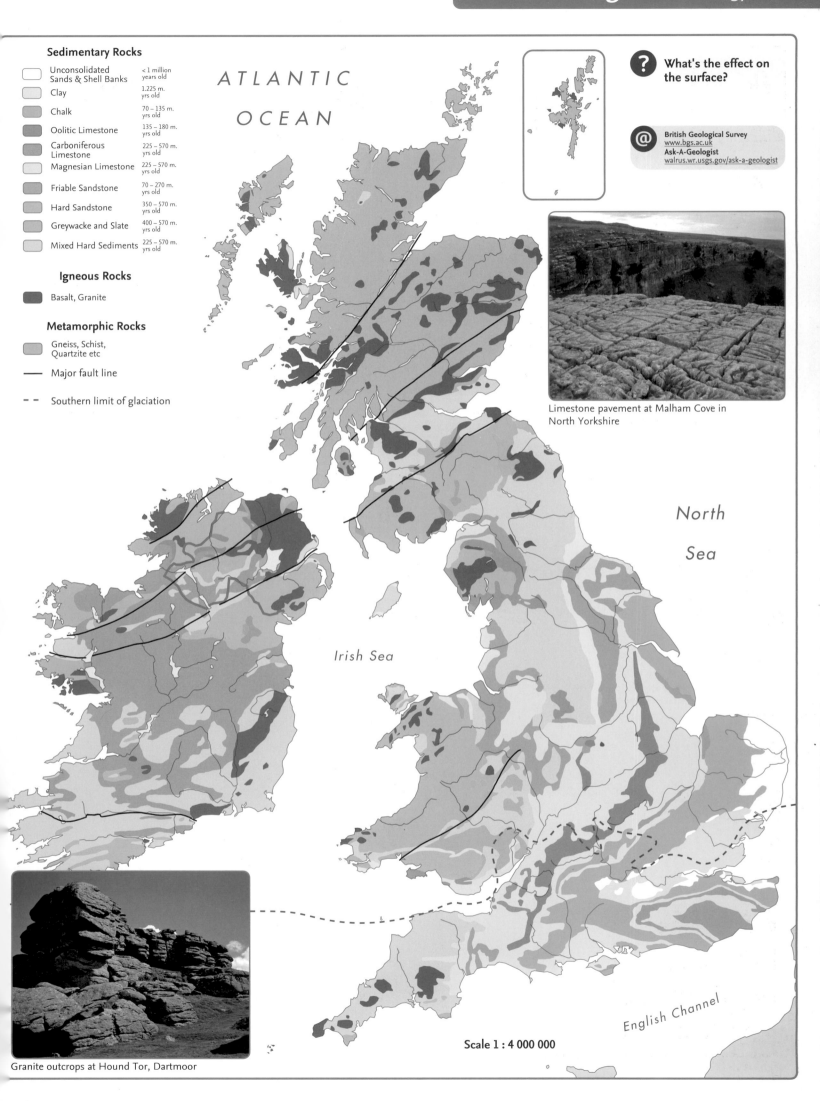

Sedimentary Rocks

	Unconsolidated Sands & Shell Banks	< 1 million years old
	Clay	1.225 m. yrs old
	Chalk	70 – 135 m. yrs old
	Oolitic Limestone	135 – 180 m. yrs old
	Carboniferous Limestone	225 – 570 m. yrs old
	Magnesian Limestone	225 – 570 m. yrs old
	Friable Sandstone	70 – 270 m. yrs old
	Hard Sandstone	350 – 570 m. yrs old
	Greywacke and Slate	400 – 570 m. yrs old
	Mixed Hard Sediments	225 – 570 m. yrs old

Igneous Rocks

Basalt, Granite

Metamorphic Rocks

Gneiss, Schist, Quartzite etc

—— Major fault line

- - - Southern limit of glaciation

ATLANTIC OCEAN

North Sea

Irish Sea

English Channel

? **What's the effect on the surface?**

@ British Geological Survey
www.bgs.ac.uk
Ask-A-Geologist
walrus.wr.usgs.gov/ask-a-geologist

Limestone pavement at Malham Cove in North Yorkshire

Granite outcrops at Hound Tor, Dartmoor

Scale 1 : 4 000 000

Annual rainfall

There is little variation between winter and summer. The highest rainfall is in the west where winds from the sea blow against the mountains and hills. Central and eastern areas are more sheltered and have lower rainfall.

Climate graphs and statistics

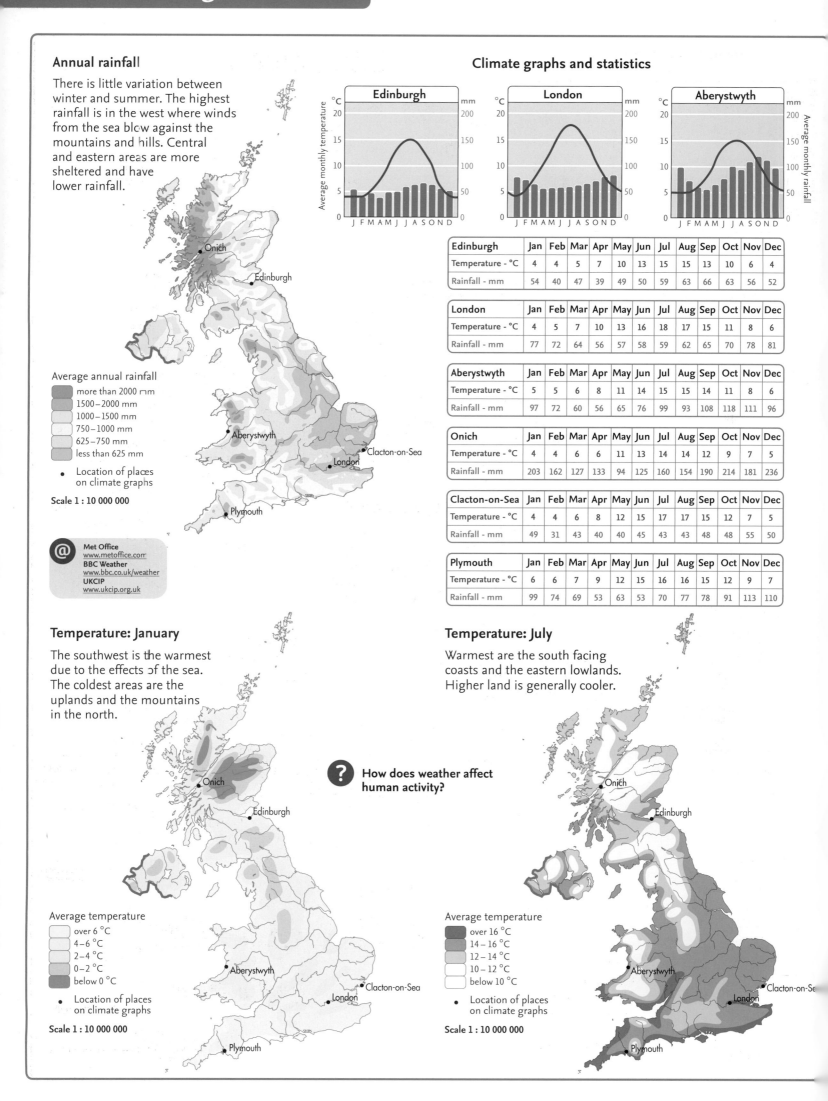

Average annual rainfall

- more than 2000 mm
- 1500–2000 mm
- 1000–1500 mm
- 750–1000 mm
- 625–750 mm
- less than 625 mm

- Location of places on climate graphs

Scale 1 : 10 000 000

Met Office
www.metoffice.com
BBC Weather
www.bbc.co.uk/weather
UKCIP
www.ukcip.org.uk

Edinburgh	Jan	Feb	Mar	Apr	May	Jun	Jul	Aug	Sep	Oct	Nov	Dec
Temperature - °C	4	4	5	7	10	13	15	15	13	10	6	4
Rainfall - mm	54	40	47	39	49	50	59	63	66	63	56	52

London	Jan	Feb	Mar	Apr	May	Jun	Jul	Aug	Sep	Oct	Nov	Dec
Temperature - °C	4	5	7	10	13	16	18	17	15	11	8	6
Rainfall - mm	77	72	64	56	57	58	59	62	65	70	78	81

Aberystwyth	Jan	Feb	Mar	Apr	May	Jun	Jul	Aug	Sep	Oct	Nov	Dec
Temperature - °C	5	5	6	8	11	14	15	15	14	11	8	6
Rainfall - mm	97	72	60	56	65	76	99	93	108	118	111	96

Onich	Jan	Feb	Mar	Apr	May	Jun	Jul	Aug	Sep	Oct	Nov	Dec
Temperature - °C	4	4	6	6	11	13	14	14	12	9	7	5
Rainfall - mm	203	162	127	133	94	125	160	154	190	214	181	236

Clacton-on-Sea	Jan	Feb	Mar	Apr	May	Jun	Jul	Aug	Sep	Oct	Nov	Dec
Temperature - °C	4	4	6	8	12	15	17	17	15	12	7	5
Rainfall - mm	49	31	43	40	40	45	43	43	48	48	55	50

Plymouth	Jan	Feb	Mar	Apr	May	Jun	Jul	Aug	Sep	Oct	Nov	Dec
Temperature - °C	6	6	7	9	12	15	16	16	15	12	9	7
Rainfall - mm	99	74	69	53	63	53	70	77	78	91	113	110

Temperature: January

The southwest is the warmest due to the effects of the sea. The coldest areas are the uplands and the mountains in the north.

? **How does weather affect human activity?**

Average temperature

- over 6 °C
- 4–6 °C
- 2–4 °C
- 0–2 °C
- below 0 °C

- Location of places on climate graphs

Scale 1 : 10 000 000

Temperature: July

Warmest are the south facing coasts and the eastern lowlands. Higher land is generally cooler.

Average temperature

- over 16 °C
- 14–16 °C
- 12–14 °C
- 10–12 °C
- below 10 °C

- Location of places on climate graphs

Scale 1 : 10 000 000

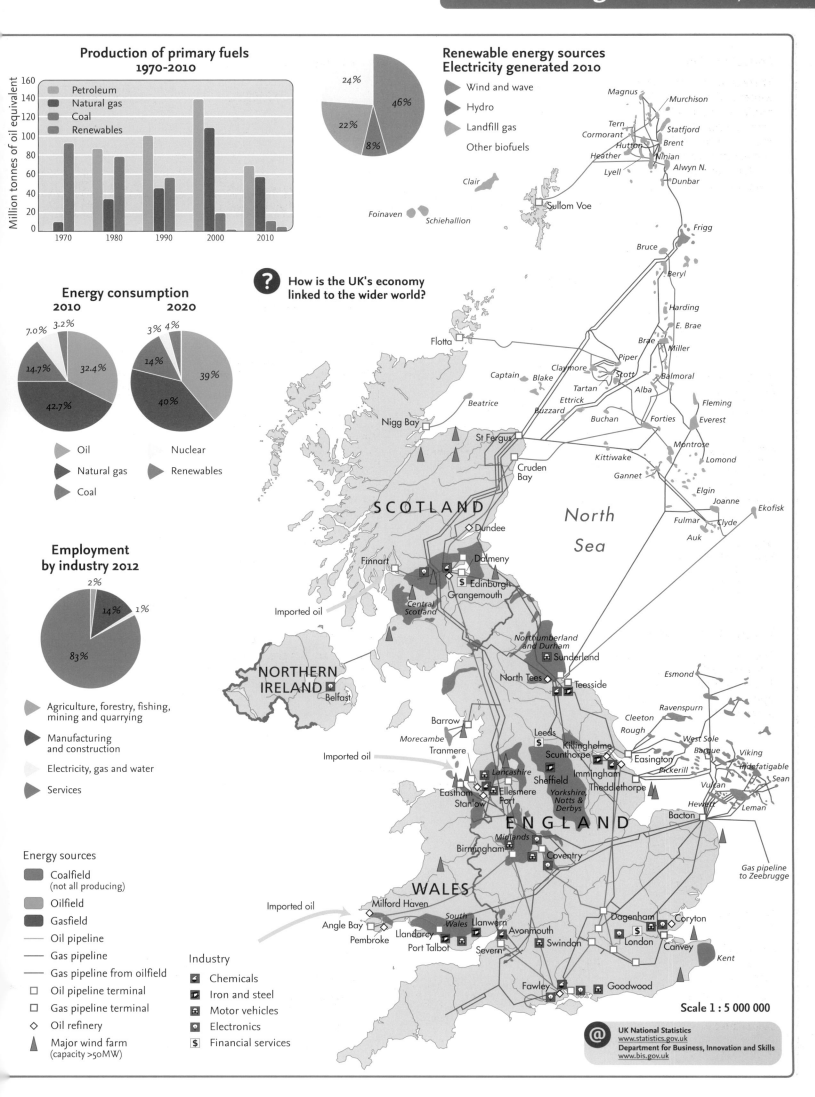

Production of primary fuels
1970-2010

Million tonnes of oil equivalent

- Petroleum
- Natural gas
- Coal
- Renewables

Renewable energy sources
Electricity generated 2010

24%
46%
22%
8%

- Wind and wave
- Hydro
- Landfill gas
- Other biofuels

Energy consumption

2010
7.0% 3.2%
14.7% 32.4%
42.7%

2020
3% 4%
14% 39%
40%

- Oil
- Natural gas
- Coal
- Nuclear
- Renewables

Employment
by industry 2012

2% 1%
14%
83%

- Agriculture, forestry, fishing, mining and quarrying
- Manufacturing and construction
- Electricity, gas and water
- Services

? How is the UK's economy linked to the wider world?

Energy sources
- Coalfield (not all producing)
- Oilfield
- Gasfield
- Oil pipeline
- Gas pipeline
- Gas pipeline from oilfield
- ▢ Oil pipeline terminal
- ▢ Gas pipeline terminal
- ◇ Oil refinery
- ▲ Major wind farm (capacity >50MW)

Industry
- Chemicals
- Iron and steel
- Motor vehicles
- Electronics
- $ Financial services

Magnus
Murchison
Tern
Cormorant
Statfjord
Hutton
Brent
Heather
Ninian
Lyell
Alwyn N.
Dunbar
Clair
Foinaven
Schiehallion
Sullom Voe
Frigg
Bruce
Beryl
Harding
E. Brae
Brae
Miller
Piper
Claymore
Stott
Balmoral
Captain
Blake
Tartan
Alba
Beatrice
Ettrick
Buzzard
Fleming
Everest
Buchan
Forties
Flotta
Nigg Bay
St Fergus
Kittiwake
Montrose
Lomond
Cruden Bay
Gannet
Elgin
Joanne
Ekofisk
Fulmar
Clyde
Auk

SCOTLAND

North Sea

◇ Dundee
Finnart
Dalmeny
Edinburgh $
Grangemouth
Central Scotland
Imported oil

Northumberland and Durham
Sunderland
North Tees
Teesside
Esmond

NORTHERN IRELAND
Belfast

Barrow
Morecambe
Tranmere
Imported oil
Leeds $
Killingholme
Scunthorpe
Immingham
Easington
Barque
West Sole
Viking
Lancashire
Sheffield
Theddlethorpe
Pickerill
Eastham
Ellesmere Port
Stanlow
Yorkshire, Notts & Derbys
Vulcan
Sean
Hewett
Leman
Bacton

Ravenspurn
Cleeton
Rough
Indefatigable

ENGLAND

Midlands
Birmingham
Coventry

WALES

South Wales
Milford Haven
Llanwern
Angle Bay
Llandarcy
Pembroke
Port Talbot
Avonmouth
Swindon
Severn
Dagenham
Coryton
London
Canvey
Kent

Imported oil

Fawley
Goodwood

Gas pipeline to Zeebrugge

Scale 1 : 5 000 000

@ UK National Statistics
www.statistics.gov.uk
Department for Business, Innovation and Skills
www.bis.gov.uk

? **Congestion and pollution – what are the answers?**

Country boundary
Internal boundary
Road
Railway
Ferry route
✈ Airport
■ Capital city
■ Regional capital
● Large town or city
○ Other town or city

Scale 1 : 4 000 000

ATLANTIC

OCEAN

North

Sea

Irish
Sea

IRELAND

NORTHERN
IRELAND

SCOTLAND

ENGLAND

WALES

English Channel

FRAN

Shetland
Islands

Lerwick

Kirkwall
Aberdeen

Stromness
Kirkwall
Thurso
Wick
Stornoway
Tarbert
Ullapool
Lochmaddy
Uig
Portree
Inverness
Lochboisdale
Aberdeen
Fort William
Tobermory
Perth
Dundee
Oban
Stirling
Glasgow
Edinburgh
Berwick-upon-Tweed
Ardrossan
Troon
Brodick
Ayr
Coleraine
Londonderry
Larne
Dumfries
Morpeth
Donegal
Cairnryan
Newcastle upon Tyne
Sunderland
Enniskillen
Stranraer
Carlisle
Durham
Belfast
Lisburn
Workington
Darlington
Middlesbrough
Ballina
Sligo
Newry
Scarborough
Westport
Dundalk
Drogheda
Douglas
Heysham
Lancaster
Harrogate
York
Kingston upon Hull
Blackpool
Bradford
Leeds
Galway
Dublin
Holyhead
Preston
Blackburn
Huddersfield
Doncaster
Grimsby
Dún Laoghaire
Bolton
Manchester
Limerick
Wicklow
Liverpool
Stockport
Sheffield
Lincoln
Tralee
Chester
Crewe
Stoke-on-Trent
Derby
Nottingham
Caernarfon
King's Lynn
Norwich
Wexford
Rosslare
Shrewsbury
Telford
Wolverhampton
Peterborough
Waterford
Aberystwyth
Birmingham
Coventry
Warwick
Northampton
Cambridge
Ipswich
Cork
Hereford
Gloucester
Oxford
Luton
Harwich
Fishguard
Pembroke
Newport
Swindon
Watford
London
Southend-on
Swansea
Cardiff
Bristol
Reading
Slough
Croydon
Bridgend
Bath
Salisbury
Crawley
Ashford
Folkestone
Taunton
Brighton
Hastings
Southampton
Portsmouth
Newhaven
Eastbourne
Weymouth
Poole
Bournemouth
Exeter
Torquay
Plymouth
Penzance

Amsterdam
Rotterdam
Zeebrugge
Channel Islands, St Malo
Roscoff Santander
Bilbao, Channel Islands, St Malo, Santander
Dieppe
Cherbourg
Le Havre
Rouen

M90, M9, M8, M74, A74 (M), A1 (M), M6, M62, M1, M2, M50, M3, M4, M18, M7, M8, M20, M9, M11, M5, M42, M40, M25, M20

Population density

The greatest concentration of population in the United Kingdom is found in the areas immediately surrounding London where the number of persons per square kilometre is more than 500 times greater than in the Scottish Highlands. The total population of England is greater than the sum of the populations of Scotland, Wales and Northern Ireland.

Persons per sq km
- over 150
- 10 – 150
- 0 – 10

Cities and towns
- over 5 000 000
- 1 000 000 – 5 000 000
- 500 000 – 1 000 000
- 100 000 – 500 000
- 20 000 – 100 000

Scale 1 : 5 000 000

**? Why do we live here?
Why do we not live there?**

Population by country
2010

- England
- Scotland
- Wales
- Northern Ireland

5% 3%
8%
84%

2010 UK total 62 262 000
2015 Projected total 64 800 000

Increase in population
1901-2031

Dotted line indicates projected population

- United Kingdom
- England
- Scotland
- Wales
- Northern Ireland

Population structure
2012

Age group
- 75 and over
- 60 – 74
- 45 – 59
- 30 – 44
- 15 – 29
- 0 – 14

Males Females

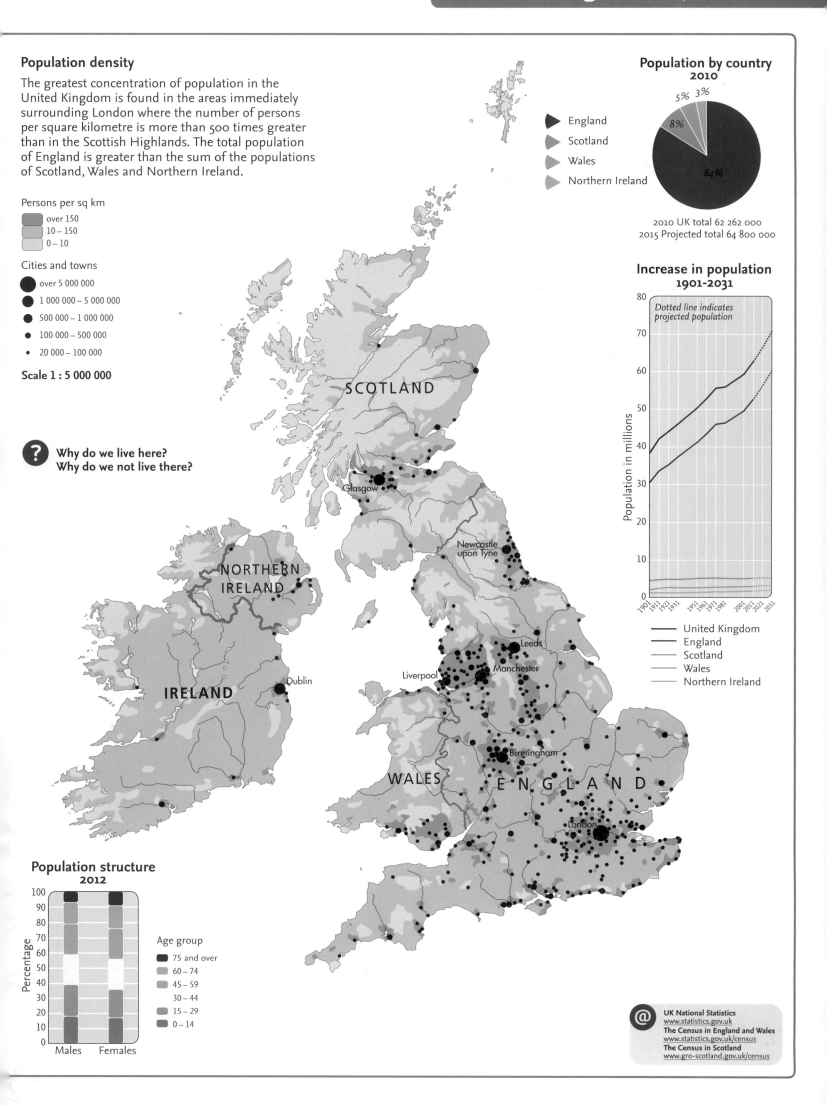

SCOTLAND

Glasgow

Newcastle upon Tyne

NORTHERN IRELAND

IRELAND

Dublin

Leeds

Liverpool Manchester

Birmingham

WALES ENGLAND

London

National Park

Area of Outstanding Natural Beauty (England, Wales & N. Ireland)
National Scenic Areas (Scotland)

Heritage Coast (England and Wales)
Preferred Conservation Zone (Scotland)

▲ World Heritage Site

● Major tourist attractions
(over 1 million visitors)

○ Other tourist attractions

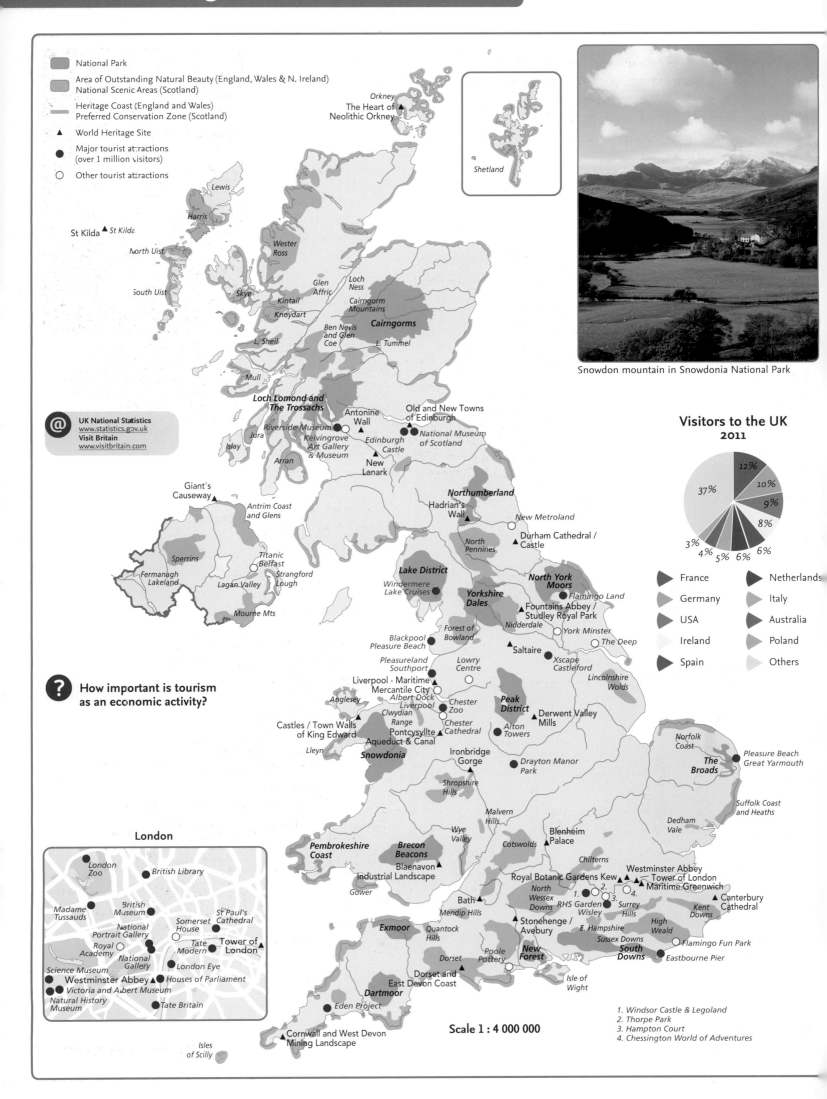

Snowdon mountain in Snowdonia National Park

@ UK National Statistics
www.statistics.gov.uk
Visit Britain
www.visitbritain.com

? How important is tourism
as an economic activity?

Orkney
The Heart of
Neolithic Orkney

Shetland

Lewis

Harris

St Kilda ▲ St Kilda

North Uist

South Uist

Wester
Ross

Skye

Glen
Affric

Loch
Ness

Kintail

Knoydart

Ben Nevis
and Glen
Coe

Cairngorm
Mountains

Cairngorms

L. Tummel

Mull

L. Sheil

Jura

Islay

Arran

Loch Lomond and
The Trossachs

Antonine
Wall

Riverside Museum
Kelvingrove
Art Gallery
& Museum

Old and New Towns
of Edinburgh

Edinburgh
Castle

National Museum
of Scotland

New
Lanark

Giant's
Causeway

Antrim Coast
and Glens

Sperrins

Fermanagh
Lakeland

Titanic
Belfast

Lagan Valley

Strangford
Lough

Mourne Mts

Northumberland

Hadrian's
Wall

New Metroland

North
Pennines

Durham Cathedral /
Castle

Lake District

Windermere
Lake Cruises

Yorkshire
Dales

North York
Moors

Flamingo Land

Fountains Abbey /
Studley Royal Park

Nidderdale

York Minster

The Deep

Forest of
Bowland

Saltaire

Xscape
Castleford

Lincolnshire
Wolds

Blackpool
Pleasure Beach

Lowry
Centre

Pleasureland
Southport

Liverpool - Maritime
Mercantile City

Liverpool
Albert Dock

Anglesey

Chester
Zoo

Chester
Cathedral

Peak
District

Derwent Valley
Mills

Clwydian
Range

Pontcysyllte
Aqueduct & Canal

Alton
Towers

Castles / Town Walls
of King Edward

Lleyn

Snowdonia

Ironbridge
Gorge

Drayton Manor
Park

Shropshire
Hills

Norfolk
Coast

The
Broads

Pleasure Beach
Great Yarmouth

Suffolk Coast
and Heaths

Malvern
Hills

Dedham
Vale

Wye
Valley

Cotswolds

Blenheim
Palace

Pembrokeshire
Coast

Brecon
Beacons

Blaenavon
Industrial Landscape

Gower

Chilterns

Royal Botanic Gardens Kew

Westminster Abbey
Tower of London
Maritime Greenwich

North
Wessex
Downs

RHS Garden
Wisley

Surrey
Hills

Canterbury
Cathedral

Kent
Downs

Bath

Mendip Hills

Stonehenge /
Avebury

E. Hampshire

High
Weald

Sussex Downs

Flamingo Fun Park

Exmoor

Quantock
Hills

New
Forest

South
Downs

Eastbourne Pier

Dorset

Poole
Pottery

Isle of
Wight

Dartmoor

Dorset and
East Devon Coast

Eden Project

Cornwall and West Devon
Mining Landscape

Isles
of Scilly

Scale 1 : 4 000 000

Visitors to the UK
2011

37%
12%
10%
9%
8%
6%
6%
5%
4%
3%

France
Germany
USA
Ireland
Spain

Netherlands
Italy
Australia
Poland
Others

London

London
Zoo

British Library

Madame
Tussauds

British
Museum

National
Portrait Gallery

Somerset
House

St Paul's
Cathedral

Royal
Academy

National
Gallery

Tate
Modern

Tower of
London

Science Museum

Westminster Abbey ▲

Houses of Parliament

London Eye

Victoria and Albert Museum

Natural History
Museum

Tate Britain

1. Windsor Castle & Legoland
2. Thorpe Park
3. Hampton Court
4. Chessington World of Adventures

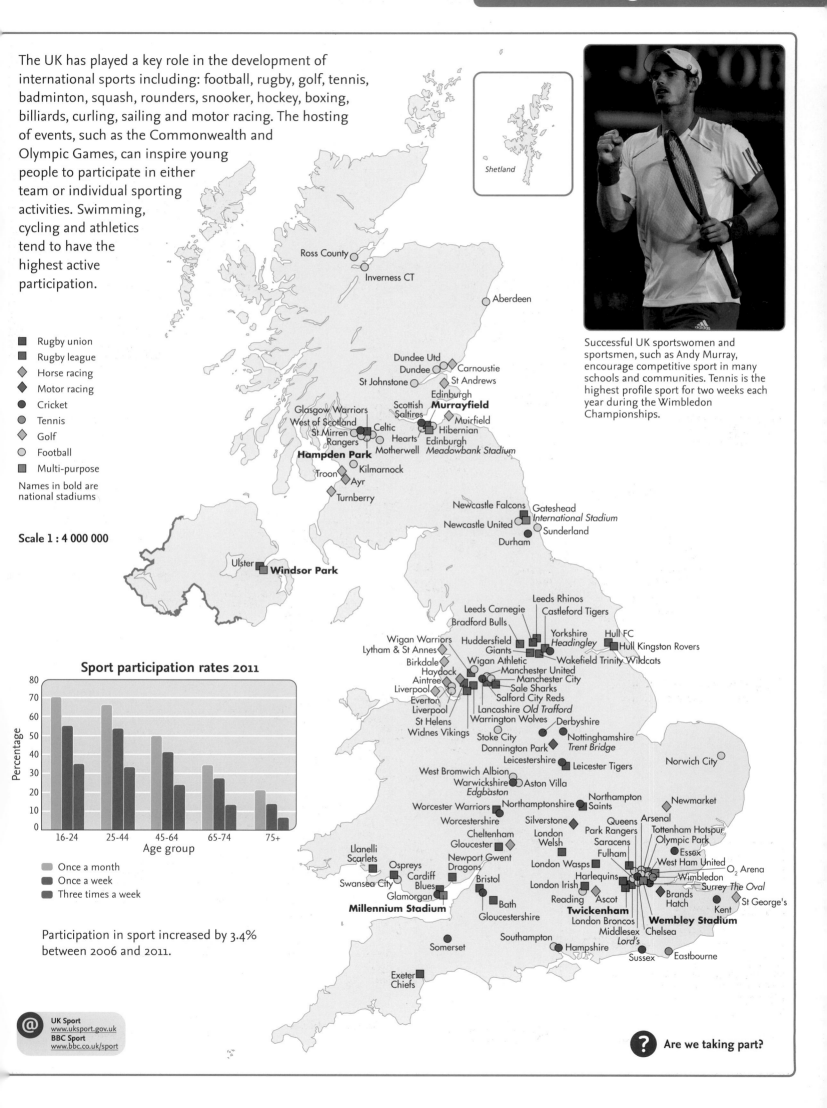

The UK has played a key role in the development of international sports including: football, rugby, golf, tennis, badminton, squash, rounders, snooker, hockey, boxing, billiards, curling, sailing and motor racing. The hosting of events, such as the Commonwealth and Olympic Games, can inspire young people to participate in either team or individual sporting activities. Swimming, cycling and athletics tend to have the highest active participation.

Successful UK sportswomen and sportsmen, such as Andy Murray, encourage competitive sport in many schools and communities. Tennis is the highest profile sport for two weeks each year during the Wimbledon Championships.

Shetland

Legend

- ■ Rugby union
- ■ Rugby league
- ◆ Horse racing
- ◆ Motor racing
- ● Cricket
- ● Tennis
- ◆ Golf
- ○ Football
- ■ Multi-purpose

Names in bold are national stadiums

Scale 1 : 4 000 000

Sport participation rates 2011

Percentage vs Age group (16-24, 25-44, 45-64, 65-74, 75+)

- Once a month
- Once a week
- Three times a week

Participation in sport increased by 3.4% between 2006 and 2011.

Map labels:

Ross County, Inverness CT, Aberdeen, Dundee Utd, Dundee, Carnoustie, St Johnstone, St Andrews, Edinburgh, Scottish Saltires, **Murrayfield**, Glasgow Warriors, Muirfield, West of Scotland, St Mirren, Celtic, Hibernian, Rangers, Hearts, Edinburgh *Meadowbank Stadium*, **Hampden Park**, Motherwell, Kilmarnock, Troon, Ayr, Turnberry

Newcastle Falcons, Gateshead *International Stadium*, Newcastle United, Sunderland, Durham

Ulster, **Windsor Park**

Leeds Rhinos, Leeds Carnegie, Castleford Tigers, Bradford Bulls, Yorkshire *Headingley*, Hull FC, Wigan Warriors, Huddersfield Giants, Hull Kingston Rovers, Lytham & St Annes, Wigan Athletic, Wakefield Trinity Wildcats, Birkdale, Haydock, Manchester United, Aintree, Manchester City, Sale Sharks, Liverpool, Salford City Reds, Everton, Liverpool, Lancashire *Old Trafford*, St Helens, Warrington Wolves, Derbyshire, Widnes Vikings, Stoke City, Nottinghamshire *Trent Bridge*, Donnington Park, Leicestershire, Leicester Tigers, Norwich City, West Bromwich Albion, Warwickshire *Edgbaston*, Aston Villa, Northampton Saints, Newmarket, Worcester Warriors, Northamptonshire, Silverstone, Queens Park Rangers, Arsenal, Worcestershire, London Welsh, Saracens, Tottenham Hotspur, Olympic Park, Cheltenham, Fulham, Essex, Gloucester, Llanelli Scarlets, Ospreys, Newport Gwent Dragons, London Wasps, Harlequins, West Ham United, O₂ Arena, Cardiff Blues, Bristol, London Irish, Wimbledon, Swansea City, Reading, Ascot, Surrey *The Oval*, Glamorgan, Brands Hatch, St George's, **Millennium Stadium**, Bath, London Broncos, Middlesex *Lord's*, Chelsea, Kent, **Twickenham**, **Wembley Stadium**, Gloucestershire, Southampton, Hampshire, Somerset, Sussex, Eastbourne, Exeter Chiefs

UK Sport
www.uksport.gov.uk
BBC Sport
www.bbc.co.uk/sport

? Are we taking part?

North Sea

ENGLAND

SCOTLAND

NORTHERN IRELAND

IRELAND

Irish Sea

North Channel

Pennines

Southern Uplands

Cheviot Hills

Lake District

North York Moors

Firth of Forth

Firth of Tay

Firth of Lorn

Firth of Clyde

Solway Firth

Morecambe Bay

Caernarfon Bay

The Wash

Humber

Isle of Man

N

W — E

S

Cromer
Skegness
Boston
The Wash
Louth
Cleethorpes
Grimsby
Spurn Head
Kingston upon Hull
Beverley
Bridlington
Flamborough Head
Scarborough
Whitby
Goole
Scunthorpe
Lincoln
Witham
Trent
Derwent
Nottingham
Mansfield
Chesterfield
Sheffield
Rotherham
Doncaster
Selby
York
Ouse
Nidd
Harrogate
Ure
Ripon
Swale
Leeds
Bradford
Halifax
Huddersfield
Barnsley
Skipton
High Peak
Macclesfield
Stoke-on-Trent
Crewe
Stockport
Manchester
Oldham
Rochdale
Bolton
Burnley
Blackburn
Preston
Wigan
St Helens
Warrington
Ellesmere Port
Chester
Mold
Clwyd
Wrexham
Rhyl
Colwyn Bay
Bangor
Anglesey
Caernarfon
Snowdon 1085
Holyhead
Birkenhead
Liverpool
Formby
Southport
Blackpool
Lytham
Morecambe
Lancaster
Kendal
Windermere
Barrow-in-Furness
Scafell Pike 977
Penrith
Workington
Whitehaven
Carlisle
Longtown
Bishop Auckland
Darlington
Stockton-on-Tees
Middlesbrough
Northallerton
Hartlepool
Durham
Sunderland
South Shields
Newcastle upon Tyne
Tyne
Wear
Tees
Morpeth
Alnwick
Berwick-upon-Tweed
Coldstream
Tweed
Galashiels
Jedburgh
Hawick
Teviot
Ettrick Water
Peebles
Biggar
Moffat
Lockerbie
Dumfries
Nith
Sanquhar
Castle Douglas
Newton Stewart
Whithorn
Stranraer
Girvan
Merrick 843
Ayr
Prestwick
Irvine
Kilmarnock
East Kilbride
Hamilton
Motherwell
Glasgow
Paisley
Greenock
Clydebank
Dumbarton
Kingston
Falkirk
Stirling
Clyde
Forth
Loch Lomond
Ben Lomond 974
Callander
Loch Tay
Tay
Crianlarich
Ben More 1174
Crieff
Dunfermline
Kinross
Kirkcaldy
Ochil Hills
Perth
Dundee
Blairgowrie
Pitlochry
Forfar
Arbroath
St Andrews
Edinburgh
Dalkeith
Dunbar
Firth of Forth
Rothesay
Bute
Brodick
Arran
Campbeltown
Mull of Kintyre
Port Ellen
Islay
Jura
Colonsay
Port Askaig
Mull
Ben More 966
Tobermory
Oban
Lochgilphead
Inveraray
Loch Linnhe
Douglas
Skerries
Dún Laoghaire
Bray
Wicklow
Belfast
Lisburn
Lagan
Newtownabbey
Bangor
Larne
Downpatrick
Newcastle
Mourne Mts
Slieve Donard 852
Antrim
Antrim Hills

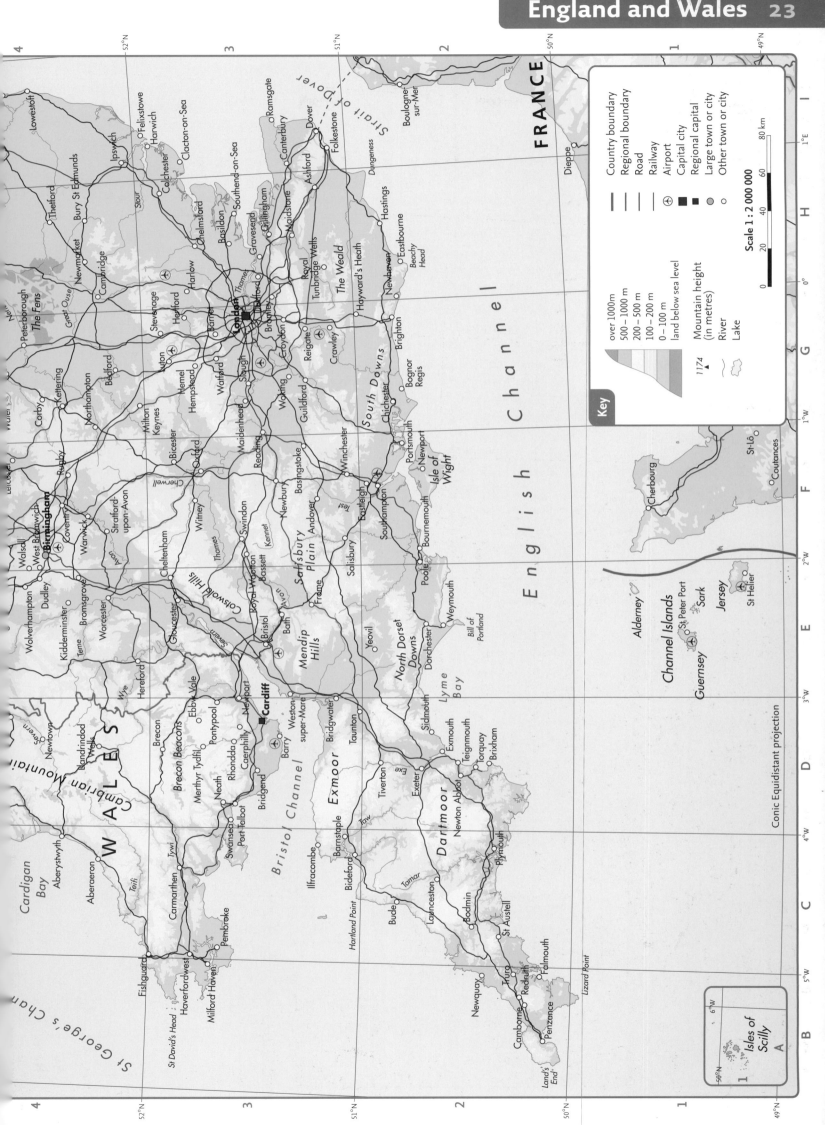

Key

Country boundary	
Regional boundary	
Road	
Railway	
Airport	⊕
Capital city	■
Regional capital	■
Large town or city	●
Other town or city	○

Scale 1 : 2 000 000

0   20   40   60   80 km

over 1000m
500 – 1000 m
200 – 500 m
100 – 200 m
0 – 100 m
land below sea level

▲ 1174   Mountain height (in metres)

River
Lake

FRANCE

Conic Equidistant projection

Conic Equidistant project

Key

over 1000m	Country boundary
500 – 1000 m	Regional boundary
200 – 500 m	Road
100 – 200 m	Railway
0 – 100 m	Airport
land below sea level	Capital city
	Regional capital
▲ 1344 Mountain height (in metres)	Large town or city
River	Other town or city
Lake	

Scale 1 : 2 000 000

0   20   40   60   80 km

Conic Equidistant projection

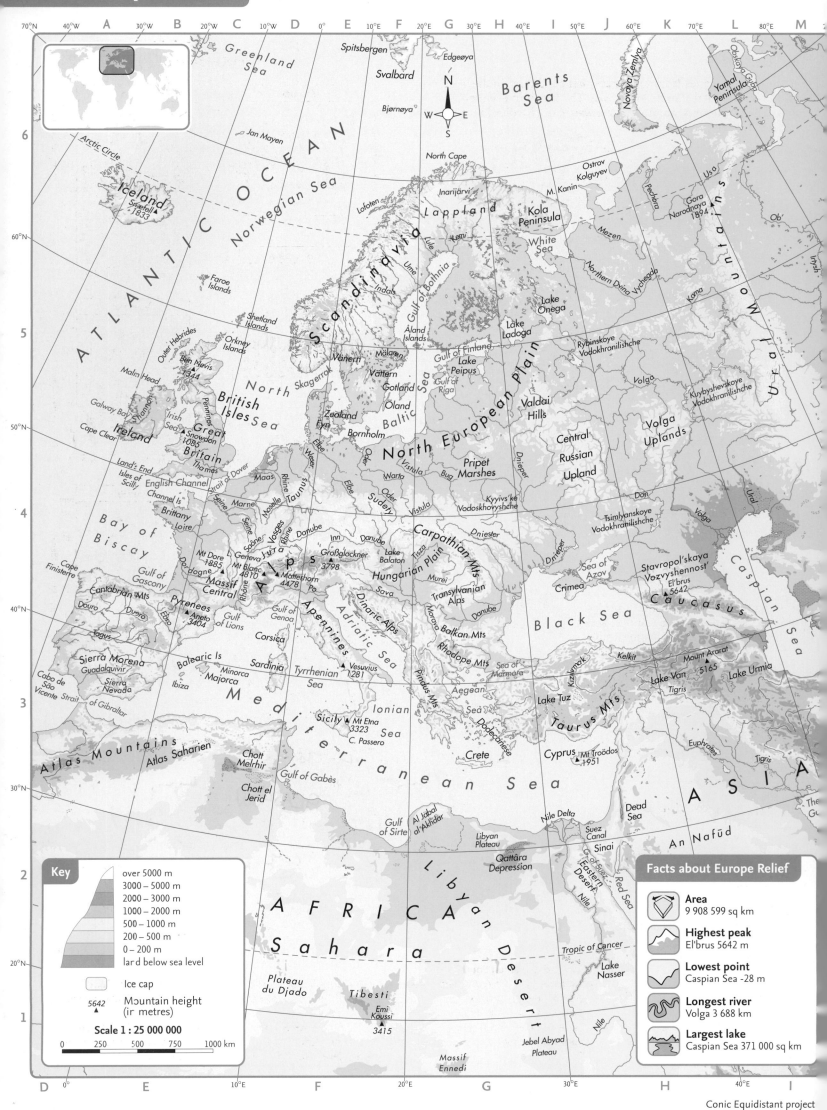

Key

- over 5000 m
- 3000 – 5000 m
- 2000 – 3000 m
- 1000 – 2000 m
- 500 – 1000 m
- 200 – 500 m
- 0 – 200 m
- land below sea level

Ice cap

5642 ▲ Mountain height (in metres)

Scale 1 : 25 000 000

0   250   500   750   1000 km

Facts about Europe Relief

Area
9 908 599 sq km

Highest peak
El'brus 5642 m

Lowest point
Caspian Sea -28 m

Longest river
Volga 3 688 km

Largest lake
Caspian Sea 371 000 sq km

Conic Equidistant project

Climate zones

Europe's climate varies from temperate, wet conditions in the west, to a drier continental climate in the east. The far north experiences sub-arctic conditions in contrast to the warm, dry Mediterranean climate of the south.

Scale 1 : 45 000 000

Semi-arid	Temperate	Mountain
Mediterranean	Continental cool summer	Sub-arctic
Wet subtropical	Continental warm summer	Tundra

Climate graphs

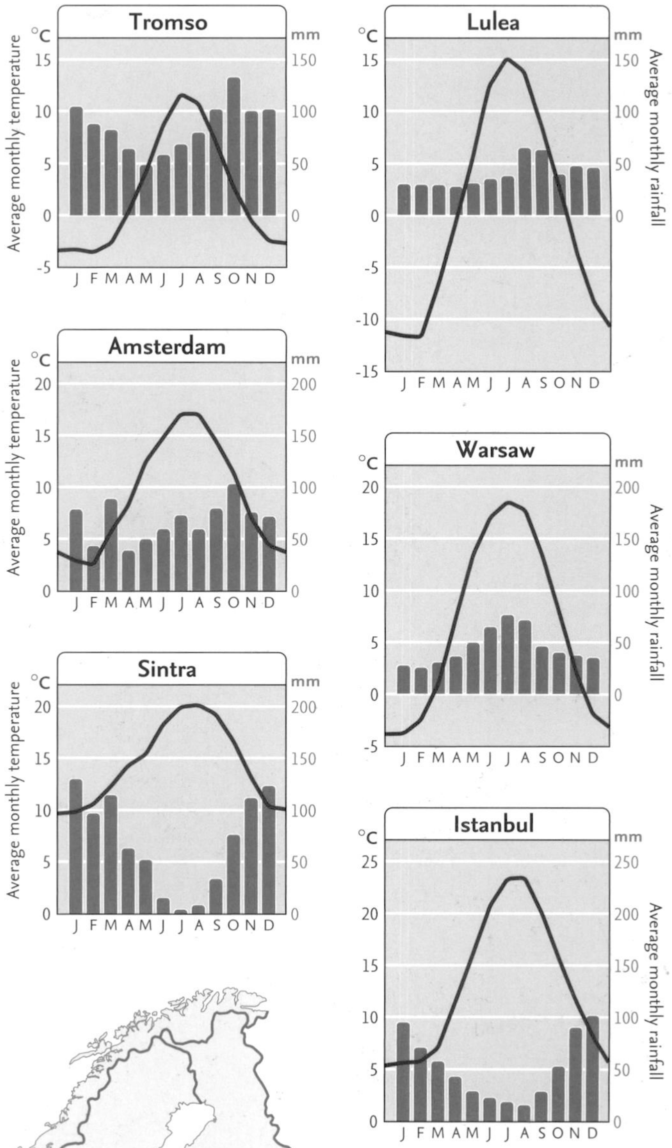

Effects of climate change

Agroclimatic zones are areas with similar climatic and agricultural conditions, water availability and crop disease vulnerability.

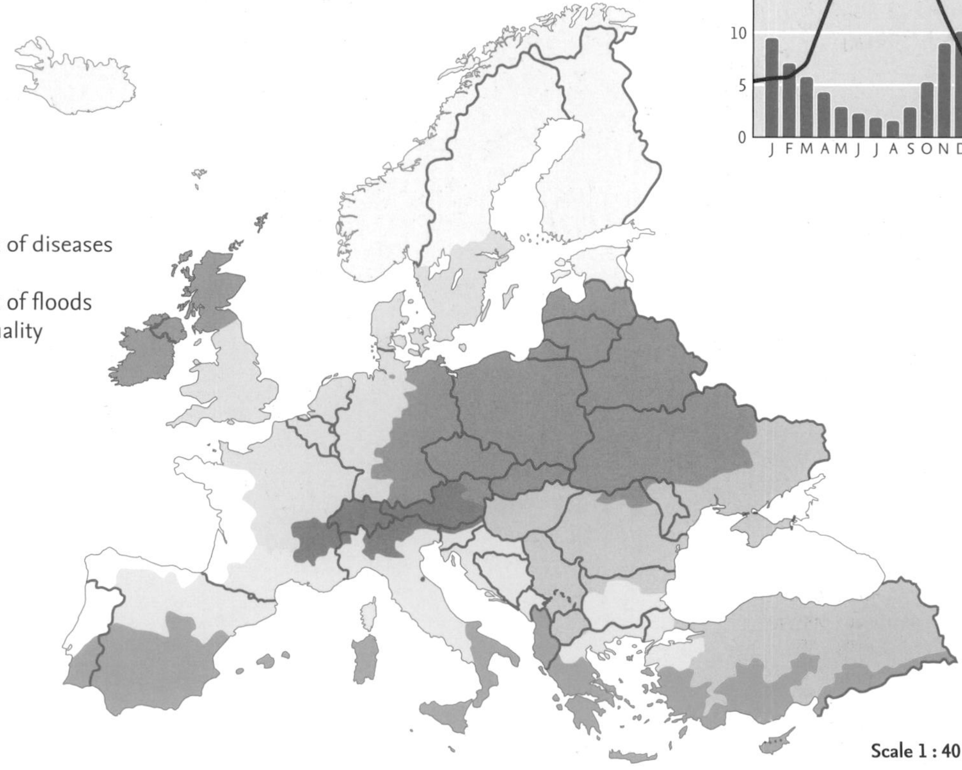

Atlantic North
- Increased risk of drought
- Sea level rise

Atlantic Central
- Increased risk of diseases and pests
- Increased risk of floods and drought
- Sea level rise

Atlantic South
- Increased risk of diseases and pests
- Increased risk of drought
- Sea level rise

Alpine
- Increased risk of floods and drought
- Poor soil quality
- Loss of glaciers and permafrost

Boreal
- Increased risk of diseases and pests
- Increased risk of floods
- Poorer soil quality
- Sea level rise

Mediterranean North
- Increased risk of diseases and pests
- Increased risk of drought
- Increased need for irrigation
- Poor soil quality
- Sea level rise

Mediterranean South
- Increased risk of diseases and pests
- Decline in crop quality
- Increased risk of drought
- Increased need for irrigation
- Poor soil quality
- Sea level rise

Continental North
- Increased risk of diseases and pests
- Increased risk of floods and drought
- Sea level rise

Continental South
- Increased risk of diseases and pests
- Increased risk of drought
- Increased need for irrigation
- Poor soil quality

Scale 1 : 40 000 000

A B C D E F G H I J K L M
40°W 30°W 20°W 10°W 0° 10°E 20°E 30°E 40°E 50°E 60°E 70°E 80°E 70°E

70°N

GREENLAND

ATLANTIC OCEAN

Barents Sea

6

Arctic Circle

ICELAND
Reykjavik

Norwegian Sea

N
W E
S

5
60°N

NORWAY

SWEDEN

FINLAND

RUSSIAN

Oslo
Stockholm

Helsinki
Tallinn
St Petersburg

FEDERATION

North Sea

Edinburgh
Belfast

ESTONIA

LATVIA
Rīga

Moscow

IRELAND
Dublin

UNITED
KINGDOM

DENMARK
Copenhagen

LITHUANIA
Vilnius

Minsk

Volga

KAZAKHSTAN

50°N

Cardiff

London
Hague

NETH.
Amsterdam

Berlin

RUS.
FED.

BELARUS

Volgograd

The
Brussels
BEL.
Luxembourg
LUX.

GERMANY

Rhine

POLAND
Warsaw

Prague

Kiev

4

Paris
Seine

CZECH
REPUBLIC

UKRAINE

Bay of Biscay

Munich

SLOVAKIA

Caspian

FRANCE
Bern
Lyon
SW.

L.

Vienna
AUSTRIA

Bratislava

Budapest
HUNGARY

MOLDOVA
Chișinău

Odesa

Sea

40°N

Milan

Ljubljana
SL.

Zagreb
CROATIA

ROMANIA

GEORGIA

SAN
MARINO

B.H.

Belgrade

Bucharest

AZERBAIJAN

PORTUGAL

MONACO

ITALY

Sarajevo

SERBIA

Danube

Black Sea

ARMENIA
AZ.

Andorra
la Vella
A.

MO.
Podgorica
K.
Priština

BULGARIA

Lisbon

Madrid

Rome

Sofia

Barcelona

Tiranë
MAC.

Skopje

İstanbul

SPAIN

ALBANIA

Ankara

IRAN

30°N

Gibraltar (UK)

GREECE

TURKEY

MOROCCO

Mediterranean Sea

Athens

Valletta

Nicosia

SYRIA

MALTA

CYPRUS

LEBANON

IRAQ

TUNISIA

ISRAEL
JORDAN

KUWAIT

3

2

ALGERIA

LIBYA

EGYPT

SAUDI
ARABIA

20°N

CHAD

Key

Country boundary
Disputed boundary
■ Capital city
○ Important city

Scale 1 : 25 000 000

0 250 500 750 1000 km

Country abbreviations
A. ANDORRA
B.H. BOSNIA-HERZEGOVINA
BEL. BELGIUM
K. KOSOVO
L. LIECHTENSTEIN
LUX. LUXEMBOURG
MAC. MACEDONIA (FYROM)
MO. MONTENEGRO
NETH. NETHERLANDS
RUS. FED. RUSSIAN FEDERATION
SL. SLOVENIA
SW. SWITZERLAND

Facts about Europe countries
(excluding Russian Federation)

Population
596 463 000

Largest Country
Ukraine 603 700 sq km

Largest City
İstanbul 12 459 000

Country with most people
Germany 82 163 000

1

D 0° E 10°E F 20°E G 30°E H 40°E I

European Union members

The European Union (EU) was created in 1957 by the Treaty of Rome. The original members of the then European Economic Community (EEC) were Belgium, France, West Germany, Italy, Luxembourg and the Netherlands. Since 1957 the EU has grown and now has 28 member states. The total population of the EU is now over 500 million.

EU original member
EU member
EU applicant
Non EU member

B.-H. BOSNIA-HERZEGOVINA
KOS. KOSOVO
L. LIECHTENSTEIN
LUX. LUXEMBOURG
MAC. MACEDONIA
MOL. MOLDOVA
MON. MONTENEGRO
R.F. RUSSIAN FEDERATION
SL. SLOVENIA
SWITZ. SWITZERLAND

Brussels
Headquarters of the European Commission and Council of the European Union

Luxembourg
Judicial centre of the EU

Strasbourg
Seat of the European Parliament for the EU

Austria 1995	Italy 1957
Belgium 1957	Latvia 2004
Bulgaria 2007	Lithuania 2004
Croatia 2013	Luxembourg 1957
Cyprus 2004	Malta 2004
Czech Republic 2004	Netherlands 1957
Denmark 1973	Poland 2004
Estonia 2004	Portugal 1986
Finland 1995	Romania 2007
France 1957	Slovakia 2004
Germany 1957	Slovenia 2004
Greece 1981	Spain 1986
Hungary 2004	Sweden 1995
Ireland 1973	United Kingdom 1973

@ European Union europa.eu   European Parliament www.europarl.europa.eu

EU migration

Europeans have a long history of migration and although many emigrate to outside of Europe there is an increase in movement within the EU zone. EU citizens can travel, work and live in other member states with few restrictions. Most states have abolished passport and customs checks between members.

Euro countries

In 2002 **euro (€)** bank notes and coins were introduced and 19 member states (the Eurozone) now use the **euro** as their official currency. There are 7 denominations of notes and 8 coins. It is likely that more members will adopt the **euro** in the future.

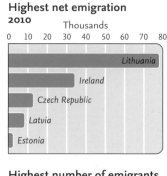

Highest net immigration
2010
Thousands
0 50 100 150 200 250 300 350 400
Italy
UK
Germany
Belgium
France

Highest net emigration
2010
Thousands
0 10 20 30 40 50 60 70 80
Lithuania
Ireland
Czech Republic
Latvia
Estonia

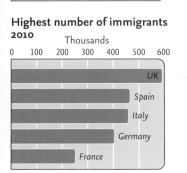

Highest number of immigrants
2010
Thousands
0 100 200 300 400 500 600
UK
Spain
Italy
Germany
France

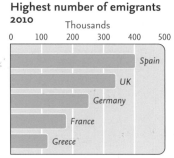

Highest number of emigrants
2010
Thousands
0 100 200 300 400 500
Spain
UK
Germany
France
Greece

Eurozone
Non Eurozone
Non EU member

A 30°W 70°N 20°W **B** 10°W **C** 0° **D** 10°E **E** 20°E **F** 30°E **G** 40°

GREENLAND
(Denmark)

Denmark
Arctic Circle
Strait

Jan Mayen

North
Cape

Barents Sea

ATLANTIC OCEAN

Norwegian Sea

Tromsø
Inarijärvi
Murmansk
Ozero Ekostrovskaya
Imandra

5

ICELAND
Reykjavik
Snæfell
1833

Fontur

60°N

Faroe
Islands

Shetland
Islands

Lofoten
Vestfjorden

N
O
R
W
A
Y

Lule
Kemi
Tornio

Lappland

Oulu

Scandinavia

Gulf of Bothnia

FINLAND

Tampere

Lake
Ladoga

Trondheim

Indals
Ume

S
W
E
D
E
N

Bergen

Orkney
Islands

Outer Hebrides

Stavanger

Ben Nevis
1344

Glasgow
Edinburgh

Malin Head

IRELAND

Galway Bay

Shannon

Dublin

Irish Sea

Belfast

UNITED

Newcastle
upon Tyne

Pennines

Liverpool
Manchester

Cape Clear
Cork

Snowdon
1085

Birmingham

KINGDOM
Cardiff

The Wash

Thames

Plymouth
Land's End
Isles
of Scilly

London
Dover

Calais
Lille

Skagerrak

Oslo

Åland
Islands

Uppsala

Vänern

Mälaren

Stockholm

Vättern

Gothenburg

Öland

Turku

Gulf of Finland

Helsinki

Hiiumaa

ESTONIA

Tallinn

Lake
Peipus

St Peter

DENMARK

Kattegat

Ärhus

Copenhagen

Zealand

Kiel
Rostock

Gotland

Saaremaa

Baltic Sea

Gulf
of Riga

North European Plain

Riga

LATVIA

LITHUANIA

Kaunas
Vilnius

Minsk

BELARUS

Malmö
Bornholm

Gdańsk

Toruń
Vistula

Poznań

Bug

Pripet
Marshes

Baranavichy

Hamburg

Bremen

Hannover

Berlin

Oder

Warta
Łódź

Warsaw

Brest

Luts'k

Kyyivs'k
Vodoskhovyshche

North
Sea

Weser
Elbe

Essen
Dortmund
Düsseldorf
Cologne
Bonn

Leipzig

Dresden

GERMANY

Frankfurt

Elbe

POLAND

Wrocław

Sudety

Prague

Katowice

Kraków

Lublin

L'viv

UKR

Zhytomyr
Ternopil'
Kie

Vodoskhovyshche

NETH.
The Hague
Amsterdam
Rotterdam

Brussels
BELGIUM

LUX.

Luxembourg

Moselle

CZECH REPUBLIC

Brno

SLOVAKIA

Dniester

A. ANDORRA
KOS. KOSOVO
L. LIECHTENSTEIN
LUX. LUXEMBOURG
M. MONACO
MON. MONTENEGRO
NETH. NETHERLANDS
S.M. SAN MARINO

English Channel

Channel Islands

Le Havre

Seine

Reims
Marne

Rhine

Nuremberg

Stuttgart

Strasbourg
Danube

Inn

Munich

Bratislava

Vienna

AUSTRIA

Danube

Tisza

Budapest

Carpathian Mountains

MOLDOVA

Chiş

Iaşi

ROMANIA

Galaţi

Brest
Brittany

Nantes

Paris

Orléans
Tours

Dijon

FRANCE

Loire

Nancy

Basel

Bern
SWITZ.

Zürich

L
Großglockner
3798

Lake
Balaton

HUNGARY

Hungarian Plain

Mureş

Transylvanian Alps

Bay of
Biscay

Allier

Bordeaux

Gulf of
Gascony

Pordogne

Dordogne

Mt Dore
1885
Massif
Central

Lyon

Mt Blanc
4810
Lake
Geneva

Matterhorn
4478

Milan

SLOVENIA

Ljubljana

Po

Venice

Zagreb

CROATIA

Sava

Drava

Belgrade

Morava

Bucharest

Danube

3

Cape Finisterre

A Coruña

Vigo

Santander
Cantabrian Mts

Gijón

León

Duero

Valladolid

Douro

Rhône

Nîmes

Toulouse

Pyrenees
Aneto
3404 A.

Marseille

Turin

Genoa

Gulf of
Genoa

M.
Ligurian
Sea

Florence

Bologna

Apennines

S.M.

Adriatic
Sea

Dinaric Alps

BOSNIA-
HERZEGOVINA

Sarajevo

SERBIA

MON.
Podgorica

Pristina
KOS

Bulkan Mts

Pindus Mts

Sofia

BULGARIA

Rhodope Mts

Istan

40°N

Oporto

PORTUGAL

Lisbon

Tagus

SPAIN

Madrid

Salamanca

Duero
Ebro

Sierra Morena

Zaragoza

Barcelona

Balearic Islands

Valencia

Minorca

Corsica

Strait of Bonifacio

Rome

ITALY

Naples

Vesuvius
1281

Sardinia

Tirana

ALBANIA

Skopje

MACEDONIA

Thessaloniki

Aegean
Sea

Cabo de
São
Vicente

Seville

Cádiz

Málaga

Sierra
Nevada

Almería

Guadalquivir

Murcia

Alicante

Ibiza

Majorca

Tyrrhenian
Sea

Isola
Stromboli

Ionian
Sea

Corfu

GREECE

Izmir

2

Tangier

Gibraltar

Algiers

Sétif

Palermo

Mount
Etna
3323

Sicily

C. Passero

Zakynthos

Patras

Athens

Naxos

Kythira

Crete

Dodecanese

Rabat

MOROCCO

Fès

Oran

ALGERIA

Tunis

TUNISIA

MALTA

C 0° **D** 10°E **E** 20°E **F**

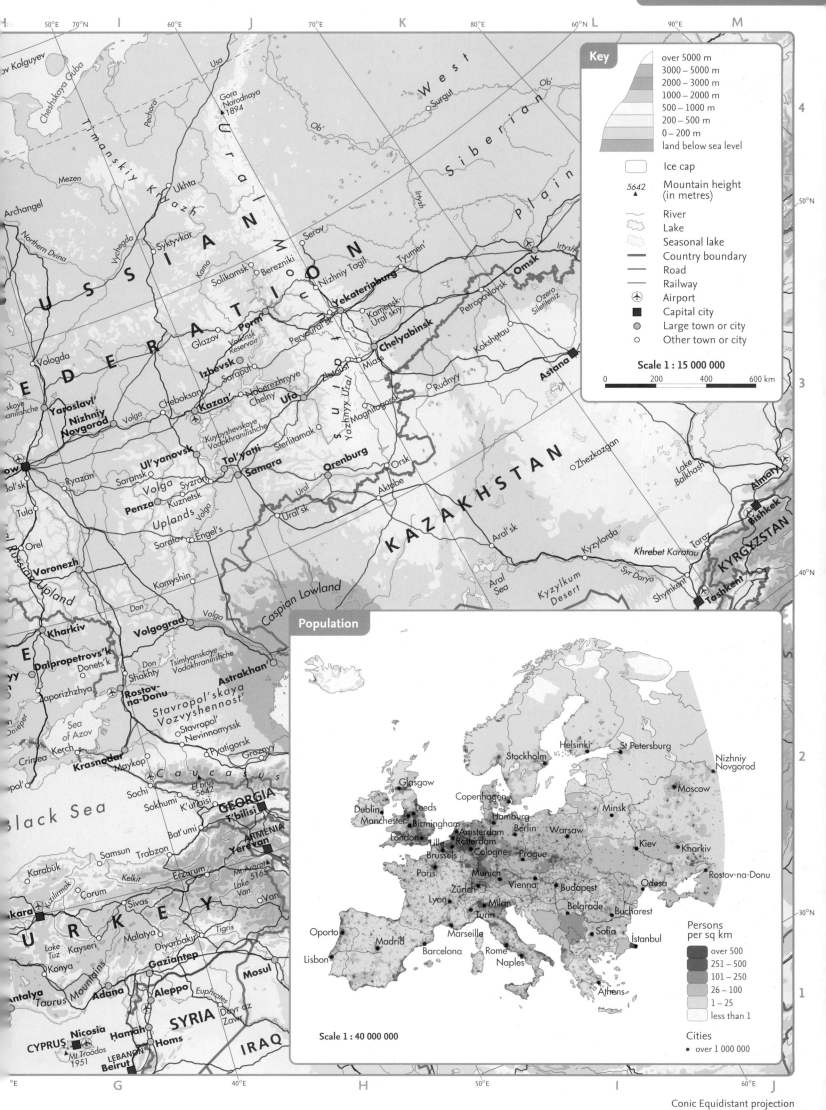

Facts about Italy

Landscape
Area: 301 245 sq km
Highest point: Mont Blanc 4810 m

Population
Total: 60 789 000
Density: 202 persons per sq km

Settlement
% Urban population: 68
Main towns: Rome, Milan, Naples, Turin

Land use
Main crops: Sugar beets, corn, grapes
Main industries: Machinery,
metal products, chemicals, food

Development indicators
Life expectancy: male 79, female 84
GNI per capita: US$ 35 330
Primary school enrolment ratio: 97
% Access to safe water: 100

Key

over 5000 m
3000 – 5000 m
2000 – 3000 m
1000 – 2000 m
500 – 1000 m
200 – 500 m
0 – 200 m
land below sea level

4810 ▲ Mountain height (in metres)

Ice cap

River
Lake
Country boundary
Road
Railway
Ferry
✈ Airport
■ Capital city
● Large town or city
○ Other town or city

Scale 1 : 5 250 000

0   50   100   150   200 km

Lambert Conformal Conic project

Italy is divided into three clearly defined physical regions, **North**, **Centre** and **South** (also referred to as the Mezzogiorno, and including the islands of Sicily and Sardinia). Each of these is subdivided into several administrative regions. More than 45% of the total population live in the North, less than 20% in Centre and 35% in the South. Economically, significant regional disparities exist between North/Centre and the South, where employment rates are noticeably lower than the national average.

Country boundary
Regional boundary
■ Capital city
○ Regional capital

The names of the regions are shown in their Italian form

Scale 1 : 6 000 000

Facts about North

Landscape
Area: 120 260 sq km
Highest point: Mont Blanc 4810 m

Population
Total: 27 763 261
Growth rate: 5.6 per 1000 people
Population over 65: 21.3 %

Land use
Arable land: 5895 sq km
Grazing land: 3779 sq km

Development indicators
Life expectancy: male 79.7, female 84.7
GDP per capita: ¤30 223
Unemployment rate: 6.7

Facts about Centre

Landscape
Area: 58 051 sq km
Highest point: Monte Vettore 2476 m

Population
Total: 11 950 322
Growth rate: 6.0 per 1000 people
Population over 65: 21.5 %

Land use
Arable land: 2176 sq km
Grazing land: 1594 sq km

Development indicators
Life expectancy: male 79.6, female 84.8
GDP per capita: ¤27 914
Unemployment rate: 8.9

Facts about South

Landscape
Area: 123 025 sq km
Highest point: Mt Etna 3323 m

Population
Total: 20 912 859
Growth rate: -0.1 per 1000 people
Population over 65: 18.2 %

Land use
Arable land: 4920 sq km
Grazing land: 8856 sq km

Development indicators
Life expectancy: male 78.8, female 83.9
GDP per capita: ¤17 417
Unemployment rate: 15.8

National Institute of Statistics
www.istat.it

Landscape

North
35%
46%
19%

Centre
9%
27%
64%

South
18%
29%
53%

Mountain
Hill
Plain

National Parks and Protected Areas have been created in Italy to preserve wildlife and natural vegetation. Most of these areas are inland. Despite its long coastline, Italy has very few protected coastal areas, with the exception of Cinque Terre Marine Protected Area which became a World Heritage Site in 1997. Pollution from oil spillage and industrial waste remains around the coast for long periods due to the low tidal movements of the Mediterranean Sea.

Alpine meadows in Gran Paradiso National Park

Air pollutants

As in other developed countries it is in the main industrial areas of Italy that most harmful substances such as oxides of sulphur and nitrogen are released into the atmosphere. The main sources of these pollutants are power stations and car exhausts.

Sources of pollutants

▶ Transport
▶ Manufacturing industries
▶ Energy combustion
▶ Other

Nitrogen oxides
1%
11%
17%
71%

Sulphur oxides
20%
46%
34%

National Institute of Statistics
www.istat.it
EUROSTAT
ec.europa.eu/eurostat
The Italian Park Portal
www.parks.it

World Heritage Site

Cinque Terre Marine Protected Area was created to protect natural features. Unique rock formations and rare species of coral are found on the seabed. It is also a sanctuary for whales.

Map labels:

Mont Blanc 4810
Val Grande National Park
Lake Maggiore
Gran Paradiso National Park
Novara
Po
Turin
Tanaro
Genoa
Cinque Terre Marine Protected Area
Cinque Terre National Park
Gulf of Genoa
Ligurian Sea
Stelvio National Park
Lake Como
Bergamo
Milan
Adda
Brescia
Oglio
Lake Garda
Trento
Dolomiti Bellunesi National Park
Piave
Padua
Venice
Adige
Po
Gulf of Venice
Trieste
Parma
Reggio nell'Emilia
Modena
Ferrara
Reno
Bologna
Ravenna
Appennino Tosco-Emiliano National Park
Forli
Rimini
Florence
Monte Falterona National Park
Ancona
Pisa
Arno
Arcipelago Toscano National Park
Ombrone
Tiber
Monti Sibillini National Park
Isola d'Elba
Grand Sasso and Monti d. Laga National Park
Pescara
Pescara
Majella National Park
Tiber
Rome
Abruzzo National Park
Gargano National Park
Ofanto
Bari
Alta Murgia NationalPark
Bradano
Brindisi
Taranto
Circeo National Park
Asinara National Park
Arcipelago de la Maddalena National Park
Olbia
Pontine Is
Naples
Vesuvius 1281
Vesuvius National Park
Cilento and Diano National Park
Pollino National Park
Gulf of Taranto
Tirso
Golfo di Orosei Gennargentu e Asinara National Park
Oristano
Sardinia
Cagliari
Tyrrhenian Sea
Sila National Park
Isola Stromboli 924
Isole Lipari
Aspromonte National Park
Ionian Sea
Palermo
Reggio di Calabria
Mt Etna 3323
Catania
Sicily
Gela
Siracusa
Isola di Pantelleria
Adriatic Sea

Legend:

■ Areas at risk from industrial pollution
□ Coastal areas most at risk from oil pollution
□ Main tourist area
■ National Park
□ Protected Area
● City with poor air quality

Scale 1 : 5 000 000

? **Protected or polluted?**

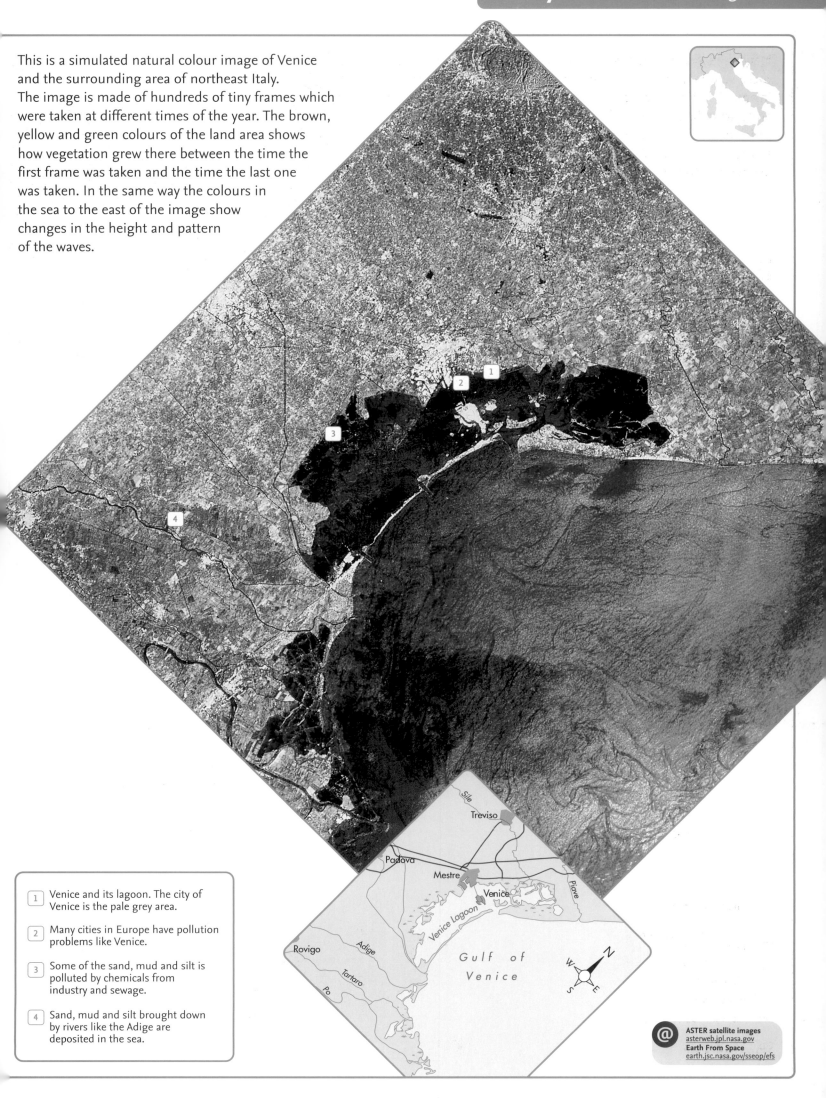

This is a simulated natural colour image of Venice and the surrounding area of northeast Italy. The image is made of hundreds of tiny frames which were taken at different times of the year. The brown, yellow and green colours of the land area shows how vegetation grew there between the time the first frame was taken and the time the last one was taken. In the same way the colours in the sea to the east of the image show changes in the height and pattern of the waves.

1   Venice and its lagoon. The city of Venice is the pale grey area.

2   Many cities in Europe have pollution problems like Venice.

3   Some of the sand, mud and silt is polluted by chemicals from industry and sewage.

4   Sand, mud and silt brought down by rivers like the Adige are deposited in the sea.

ASTER satellite images
asterweb.jpl.nasa.gov
Earth From Space
earth.jsc.nasa.gov/sseop/efs

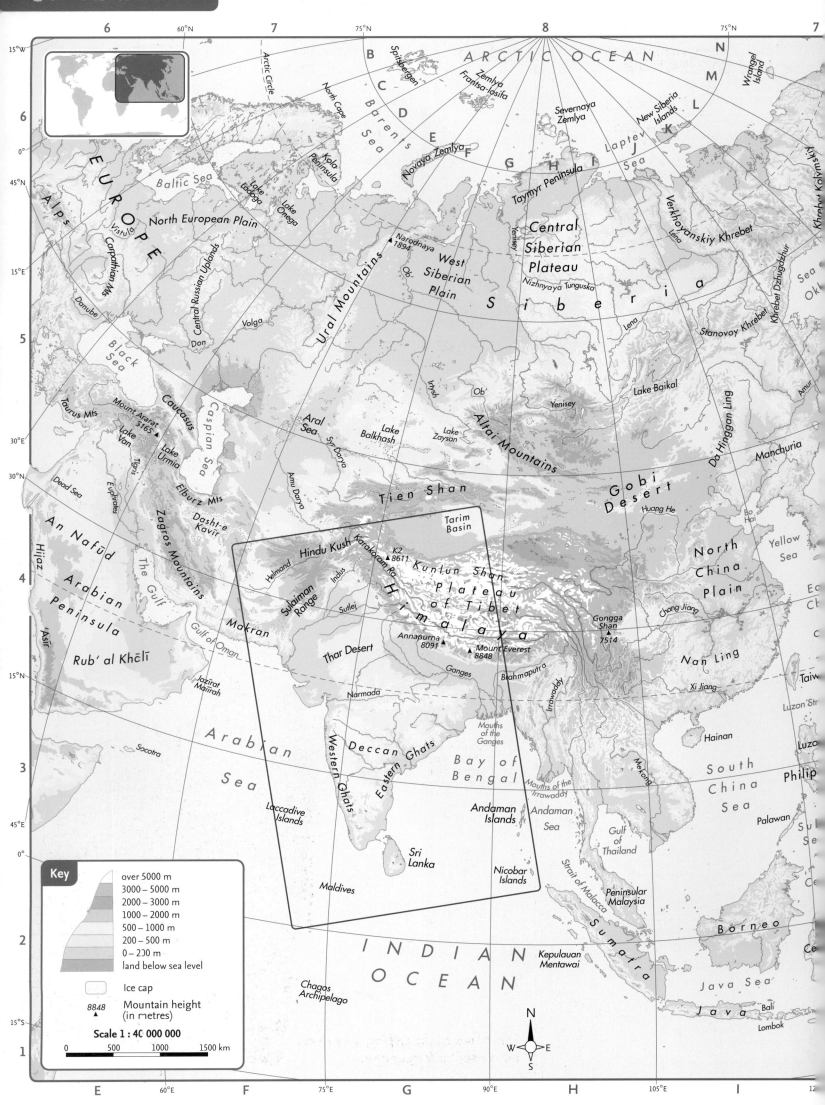

ARCTIC OCEAN

EUROPE

Alps

Baltic Sea

North European Plain

Carpathian Mts

Vistula

Danube

Lake Ladoga

Lake Onega

Kola Peninsula

North Cape

Arctic Circle

Spitsbergen

Barents Sea

Novaya Zemlya

Zemlya Frantsa-Iosifa

Severnaya Zemlya

New Siberia Islands

Wrangel Island

Khrebet Dzhugdzhur

Taymyr Peninsula

Central Siberian Plateau

West Siberian Plain

Narodnaya 1894

Ural Mountains

S i b e r i a

Verkhoyanskiy Khrebet

Lena

Nizhnyaya Tunguska

Yenisey

Ob

Irtysh

Central Russian Uplands

Volga

Don

Black Sea

Caspian Sea

Caucasus

Mount Ararat 5165

Taurus Mts

Lake Van

Lake Urmia

Elburz Mts

Aral Sea

Syr Darya

Lake Balkhash

Lake Zaysan

Ob'

Yenisey

Altai Mountains

Lake Baikal

Stanovoy Khrebet

Amur

Da Hinggan Ling

Manchuria

Dead Sea

Euphrates

Tigris

Zagros Mountains

Dasht-e Kavir

Amu Darya

Tien Shan

Gobi Desert

Huang He

Bo Hai

Yellow Sea

An Nafūd

Hijaz

Arabian Peninsula

'Asir

Rub' al Khālī

The Gulf

Gulf of Oman

Makran

Hindu Kush

Karakoram Ra.

K2 8611

Kunlun Shan

Tarim Basin

Plateau of Tibet

North China Plain

Chang Jiang

Gongga Shan 7514

Nan Ling

Helmand

Sulaiman Range

Indus

Sutlej

H i m a l a y a

Annapurna 8091

Mount Everest 8848

Ganges

Brahmaputra

Taiwan

Jazīrat Maṣīrah

Thar Desert

Narmada

Mouths of the Ganges

Irrawaddy

Xi Jiang

Luzon Str.

Hainan

Luzon

Socotra

Arabian Sea

Deccan

Western Ghats

Eastern Ghats

Bay of Bengal

Mouths of the Irrawaddy

Andaman Islands

Andaman Sea

Mekong

Gulf of Thailand

South China Sea

Philip

Palawan

Laccadive Islands

Sri Lanka

Nicobar Islands

Strait of Malacca

Peninsular Malaysia

Su Se

Maldives

Chagos Archipelago

INDIAN OCEAN

Kepulauan Mentawai

Sumatra

Borneo

Ce

Java Sea

Java

Bali

Lombok

Key

over 5000 m
3000 – 5000 m
2000 – 3000 m
1000 – 2000 m
500 – 1000 m
200 – 500 m
0 – 200 m
land below sea level

Ice cap

▲ 8848 Mountain height (in metres)

Scale 1 : 40 000 000

0   500   1000   1500 km

N
W   E
S

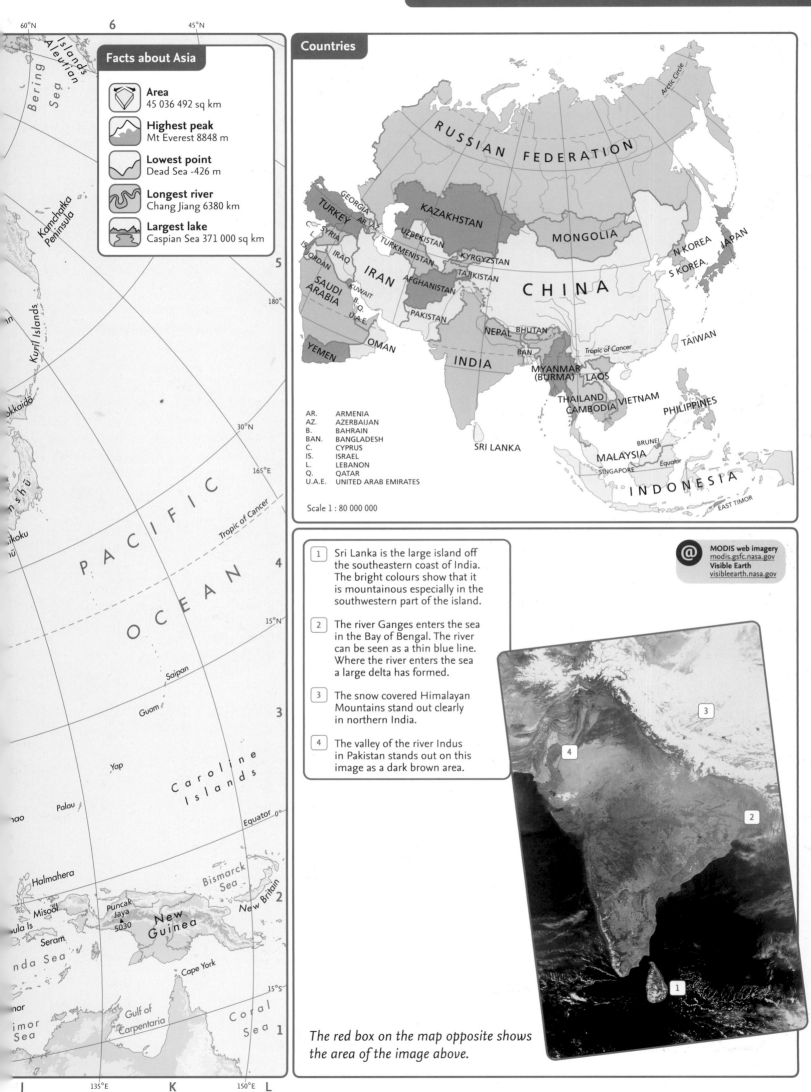

Facts about Asia

Area
45 036 492 sq km

Highest peak
Mt Everest 8848 m

Lowest point
Dead Sea -426 m

Longest river
Chang Jiang 6380 km

Largest lake
Caspian Sea 371 000 sq km

Countries

AR. ARMENIA
AZ. AZERBAIJAN
B. BAHRAIN
BAN. BANGLADESH
C. CYPRUS
IS. ISRAEL
L. LEBANON
Q. QATAR
U.A.E. UNITED ARAB EMIRATES

Scale 1 : 80 000 000

1 Sri Lanka is the large island off the southeastern coast of India. The bright colours show that it is mountainous especially in the southwestern part of the island.

2 The river Ganges enters the sea in the Bay of Bengal. The river can be seen as a thin blue line. Where the river enters the sea a large delta has formed.

3 The snow covered Himalayan Mountains stand out clearly in northern India.

4 The valley of the river Indus in Pakistan stands out on this image as a dark brown area.

@ **MODIS web imagery**
modis.gsfc.nasa.gov
Visible Earth
visibleearth.nasa.gov

The red box on the map opposite shows the area of the image above.

Lambert Azimuthal Equal Area projection

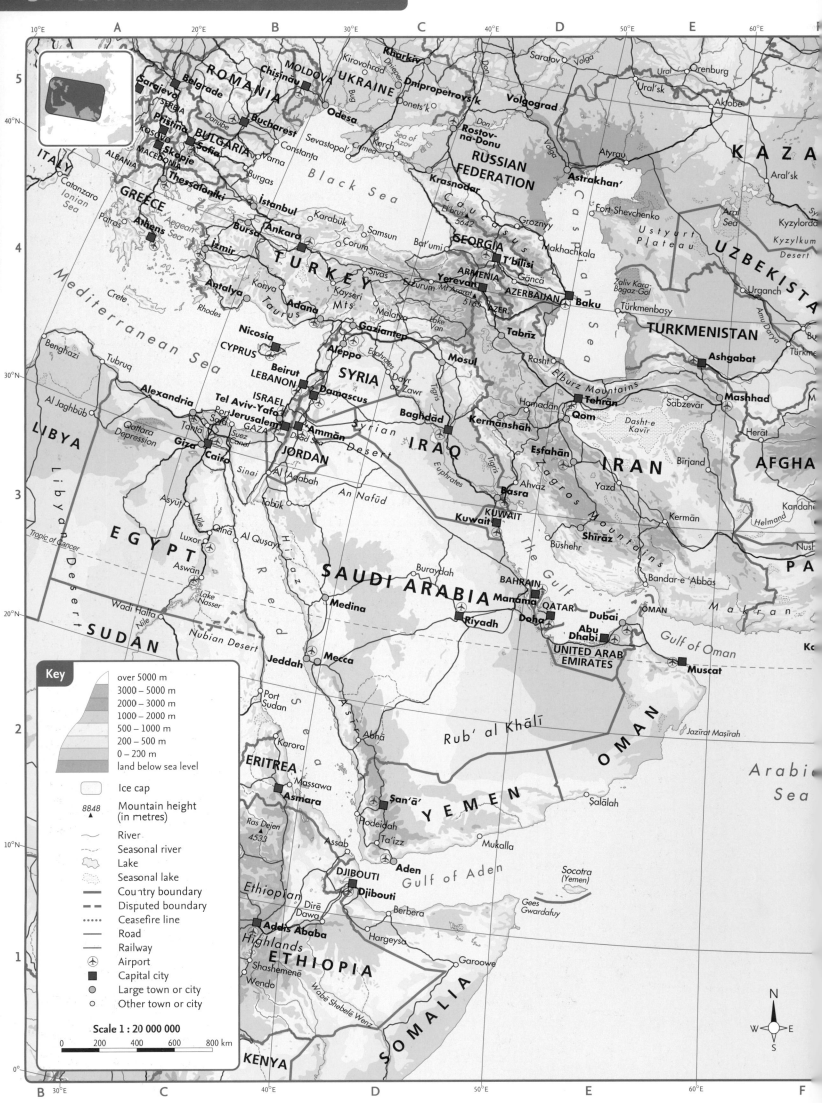

Key

	over 5000 m
	3000 – 5000 m
	2000 – 3000 m
	1000 – 2000 m
	500 – 1000 m
	200 – 500 m
	0 – 200 m
	land below sea level
	Ice cap
▲ 8848	Mountain height (in metres)
	River
	Seasonal river
	Lake
	Seasonal lake
	Country boundary
	Disputed boundary
	Ceasefire line
	Road
	Railway
✈	Airport
■	Capital city
●	Large town or city
○	Other town or city

Scale 1 : 20 000 000

0   200   400   600   800 km

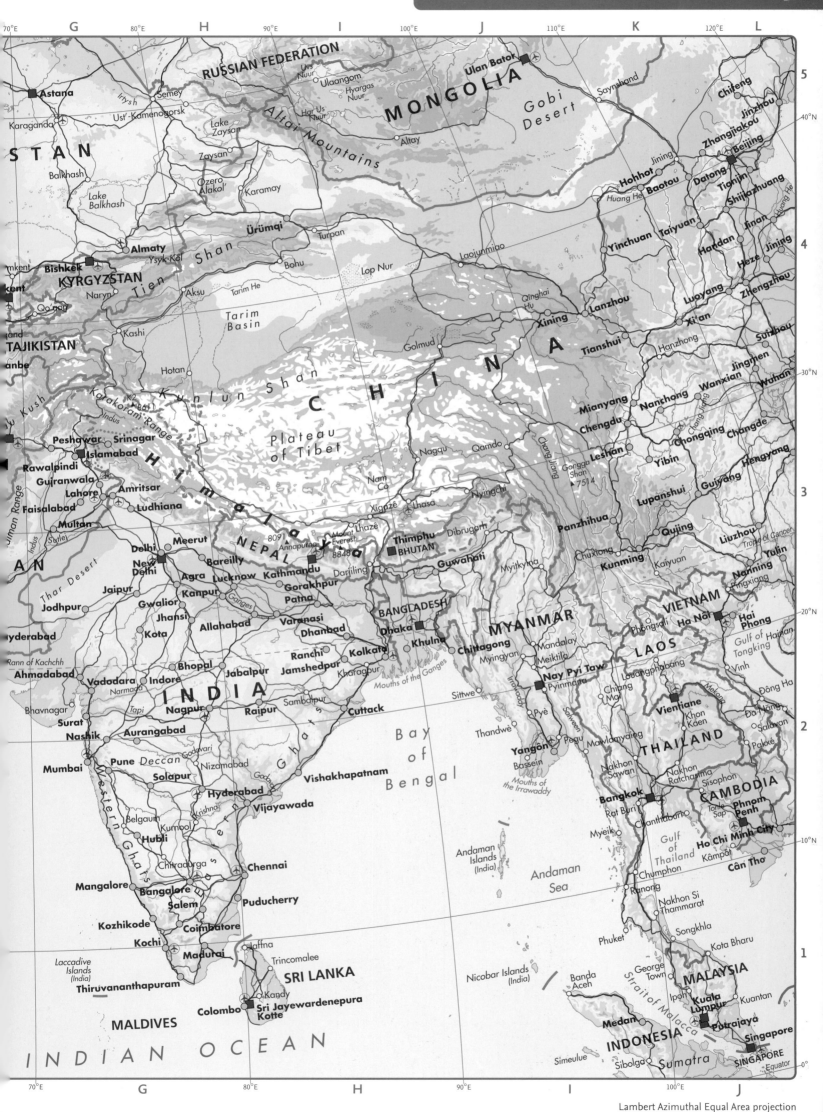

Lambert Azimuthal Equal Area projection

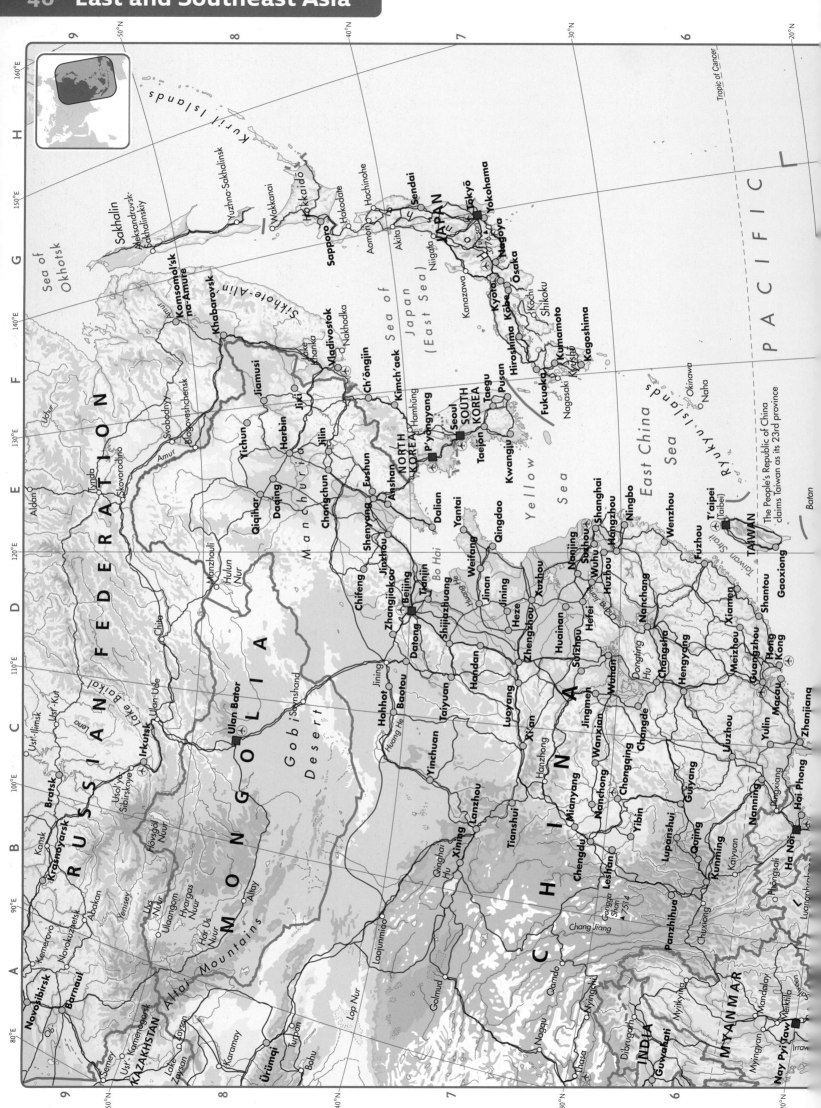

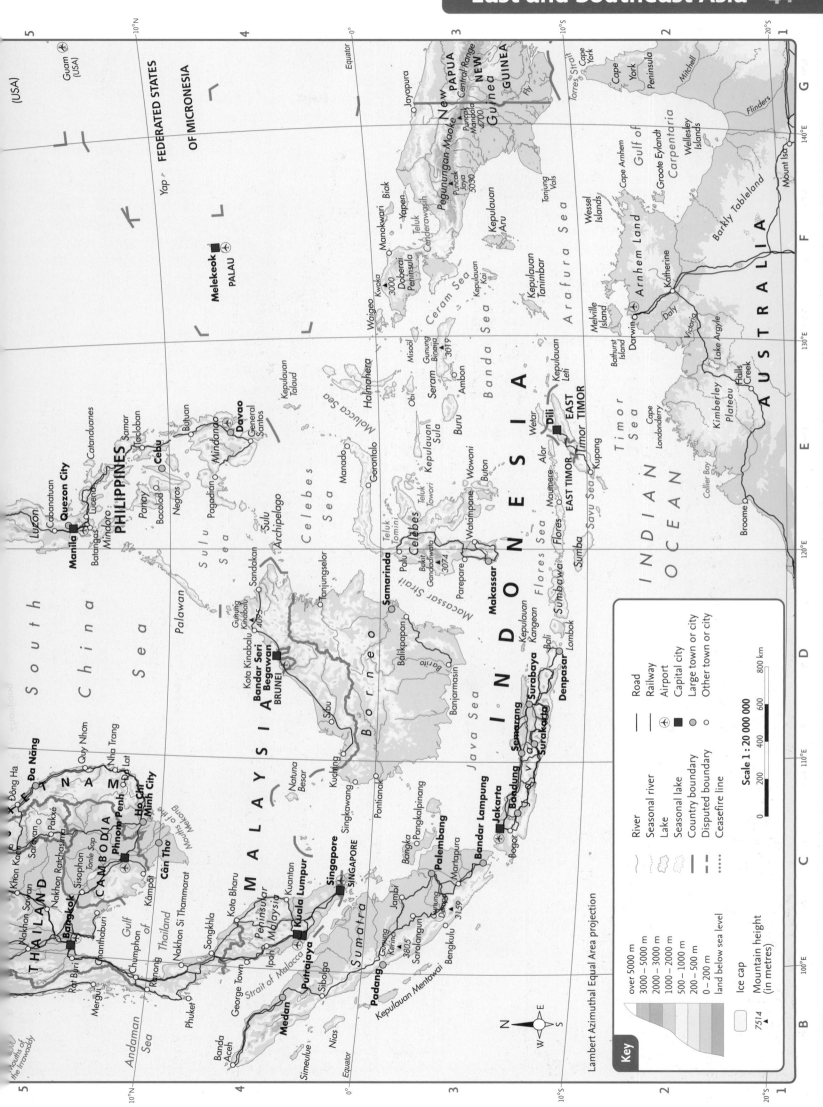

Key

	over 5000 m
	3000 – 5000 m
	2000 – 3000 m
	1000 – 2000 m
	500 – 1000 m
	200 – 500 m
	0 – 200 m
	land below sea level
	Ice cap

7514 ▲ Mountain height (in metres)

	River	Road
	Seasonal river	Railway
	Lake	✈ Airport
	Seasonal lake	■ Capital city
	Country boundary	● Large town or city
	Disputed boundary	○ Other town or city
	Ceasefire line	

Scale 1 : 20 000 000

0 200 400 600 800 km

Lambert Azimuthal Equal Area projection

AUSTRALIA

INDONESIA

PHILIPPINES

MALAYSIA

THAILAND

VIETNAM

CAMBODIA

NEW GUINEA

PAPUA NEW GUINEA

FEDERATED STATES OF MICRONESIA

PALAU

BRUNEI

EAST TIMOR

Facts about Japan

Landscape
Area: 377 727 sq km
Highest point: Fuji-san 3776 m

Population
Total: 126 497 000
Density: 335 persons per sq km

Settlement
% Urban population: 91
Main towns: Tōkyō, Ōsaka-Kōbe, Nagoya, Fukuoka-Kita-Kyūshū

Land use
Main crops: Rice, potatoes, sugar beets
Main industries: Electrical equipment, transport equipment, other machinery, chemicals

Development indicators
Life expectancy: male 80, female 86
GNI per capita: US$ 45 180
Primary school enrolment ratio: 100
% Access to safe water: 100

Key

3000 – 5000 m		
2000 – 3000 m		
1000 – 2000 m		
500 – 1000 m		
200 – 500 m		
0 – 200 m		

3776 ▲ Mountain height (in metres)
〜 River
〜 Lake

—— Country boundary
- - - Disputed boundary
····· Ceasefire line
—— Road
—— Railway
····· Ferry
✈ Airport
■ Capital city
● Large town or city
○ Other town or city

Japanese name forms

-dake	peak
-hanto	peninsula
-jima	island
-kai	bay, inlet
-kaikyo	strait
-ko	lake
-nada	sea, gulf
-retto	chain of islands
-san	mountain
-sanchi	mountainous area
-shima	island
-suido	strait, channel
-to	island
-wan	sea
-yama	mountain

Scale 1 : 7 500 000

0   100   200   300   400 km

Albers Equal Area Conic projection

Annual rainfall

The driest parts of Japan are in the north, on the island of Hokkaidō. Most rain falls on the high mountain tops and the southern and western coasts.

Average annual rainfall

- more than 3000 mm
- 2000 – 3000 mm
- 1500 – 2000 mm
- 1000 – 1500 mm
- less than 1000 mm

Scale 1 : 15 000 000

Land use

Over 66% of this steep-sided mountainous country is covered by forest. Flat land, suitable for agriculture, is in very short supply and as a result farming is intensive in order to maximise production.

- Rice
- Tea
- Mulberry
- Orchards
- Upland fields
- Forest
- Built-up

Scale 1 : 15 000 000

Land use by category

- 8%
- 1%
- 4%
- 9%
- 12%
- 66%

- Forest
- Farmland
- Built-up
- Water
- Grassland
- Other

Population

Japan has a high overall population density. There are huge contrasts in density between the land suitable for urban development and the unspoilt forested and wilderness areas in the northern islands.

Persons per sq km

- over 250
- 100 – 250
- 10 – 100
- 0 – 10

Cities

- ● over 25 000 000
- ● 10 000 000 – 25 000 000
- • 1 000 000 – 10 000 000

Scale 1 : 15 000 000

Sapporo

Sendai

Tōkyō

Kyōto
Nagoya
Yokohama
Kawasaki
Kōbe
Osaka
Hiroshima
Fukuoka

Economic activity

Tokyo and its surrounding area is the main economic heart of Japan. Electronics and car manufacturing are major industries. The primary sector of the economy is very small due to a lack of natural resources.

Industry

- Iron / Steel
- Oil refineries
- Shipbuilding
- Motor vehicles
- Mechanical engineering
- Electronics
- Publishing / Paper
- Chemicals
- Textiles / Clothing
- Food processing
- • Major industrial centre

Service industry

- Banking and finance

Scale 1 : 15 000 000

Sapporo

Niigata
Toyama
Tōkyō
Kyōto
Nagoya
Yokohama
Okayama
Kōbe
Ōsaka
Kita-Kyūshū
Ōita
Nagasaki

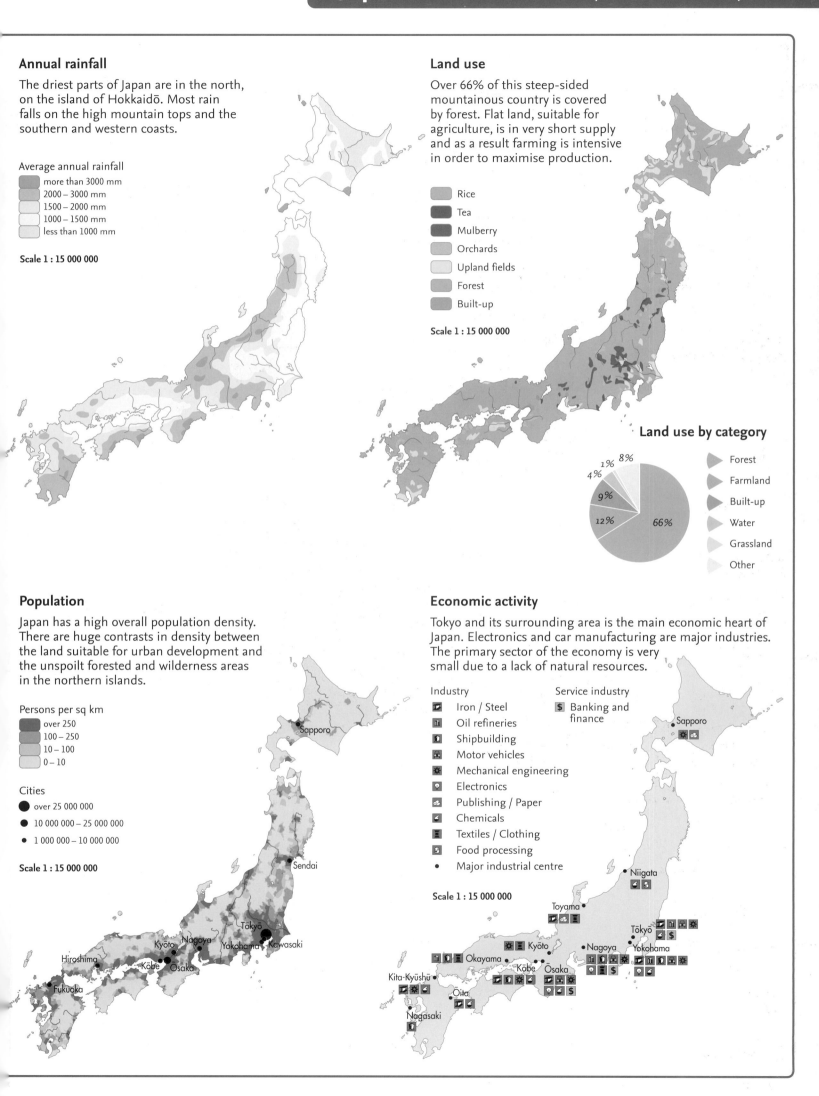

Japan is situated on the 'Ring of Fire' around the Pacific Ocean. There are almost 200 volcanoes in the 'Ring of Fire' and over 20 are still active.

Earthquakes are more disastrous than volcanic eruptions in Japan where 5000 earthquakes are recorded annually. The main earthquake zones lie on the Pacific side of Japan. Strong earthquakes may destroy roads and railways, collapse houses and result in many casualties.

Tōhoku earthquake :
The most powerful earthquake ever to hit Japan, with a magnitude of 9 on the Richter Scale, occurred in March 2011. It's epicentre was 70 km east of the Oshika Peninsula. The earthquake created huge tsunami waves that caused widespread destruction on Japan's Pacific coast. Over 15 000 people were killed as a result of the earthquake and tsunami. The tsunami also caused a number of nuclear accidents, the worst of which was in Fukushima.

Volcanic activity

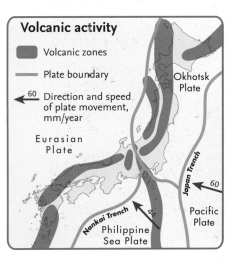

- Volcanic zones
- Plate boundary
- 60 ← Direction and speed of plate movement, mm/year

Okhotsk Plate

Eurasian Plate

Japan Trench

Nankai Trench

Philippine Sea Plate

Pacific Plate

Earthquake seismogram :
A seismogram is used to record the horizontal or vertical vibration caused during the course of an earthquake. The vertical divisions represent time intervals of 5 seconds.

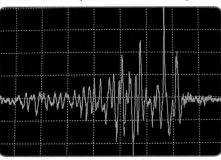

? Where do volcanoes and earthquakes occur?

- Volcanic rocks
- ▲ Active volcano (erupted since 1850)
- △ Other volcano
- ● Earthquakes greater than magnitude 6 since 1900

Scale 1 : 9 000 000

Hokkaidō

Tokachi-dake
Akan
Sapporo
Usu-zan
Komaga-take

Honshū

Iwate-san
Chokai-san
Zaō-zan
Oshika Peninsula
Azuma-san
Adatara-san

Magnitude 9.0 earthquake and tsunami 11 March 2011

Niigata-yake-yama
Hiuchiga-take
Tate-yama
Iwasuge-yama
Yake-dake
Asama

Tōkyō

Fuji
Nagoya
Izu-tobu

Kōbe

Fuji :
Situated on the island of Honshū, Fuji is a dormant volcano which has not erupted since 1707. At 3776 m, it is the highest mountain in Japan and has a crater which is 610 metres in diameter.

Shikoku

Unzen-dake
Aso-san
Kyūshū
Kirishima-yama
Kagoshima
Sakurajima

Richter Scale
The scale of measurement used to describe the strength of an earthquake is known as the Richter Scale. The scale measures the energy which is released at the centre of an earthquake. Every year about 50 000 quakes measuring 3 – 4 are recorded worldwide, while only 800 measuring 5 – 6 occur.

9	Over 8.0 most powerful earthquake
8	7.0 – 8.0 major earthquake
7	6.0 – 7.0 destructive earthquake
6	4.5 – 6.0 earthquake causes local damage
5	3.5 – 4.5 earthquake felt by many people
4	2.5 – 3.5 earthquake recorded but not felt
3	below 2.5 earthquake not recorded
2	
1	
0	

Sakurajima :
Sakurajima is an active volcano situated in Kagoshima Bay. Its eruptions are generally gentle with little explosive activity.

USGS National Earthquake Information Center
earthquake.usgs.gov/regional/neic
Earthquake Research Institute
www.eri.u-tokyo.ac.jp/eng

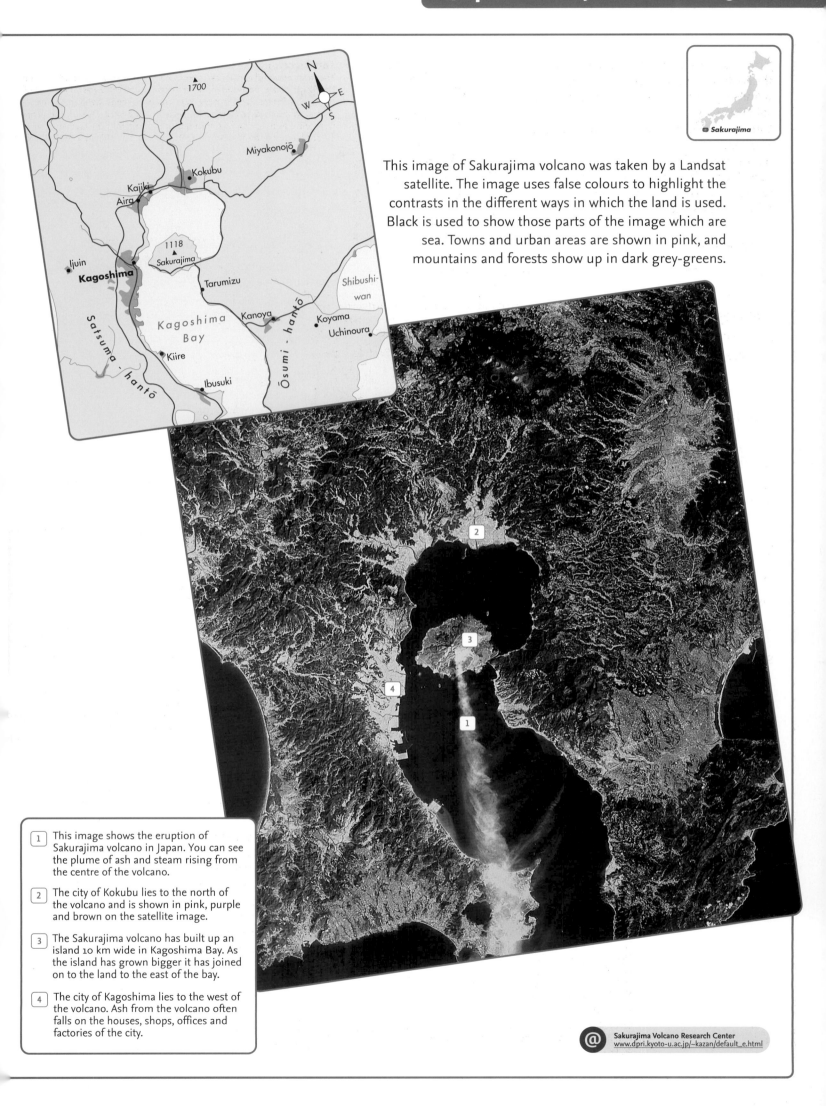

This image of Sakurajima volcano was taken by a Landsat satellite. The image uses false colours to highlight the contrasts in the different ways in which the land is used. Black is used to show those parts of the image which are sea. Towns and urban areas are shown in pink, and mountains and forests show up in dark grey-greens.

1700

Miyakonojō

Kokubu

Kajiki
Aira

1118
Sakurajima

Ijuin

Kagoshima

Tarumizu

Shibushi-wan

Kanoya

Koyama
Uchinoura

Kagoshima
Bay

Satsuma - hantō

Ōsumi - hantō

Kiire

Ibusuki

🔲 *Sakurajima*

1. This image shows the eruption of Sakurajima volcano in Japan. You can see the plume of ash and steam rising from the centre of the volcano.

2. The city of Kokubu lies to the north of the volcano and is shown in pink, purple and brown on the satellite image.

3. The Sakurajima volcano has built up an island 10 km wide in Kagoshima Bay. As the island has grown bigger it has joined on to the land to the east of the bay.

4. The city of Kagoshima lies to the west of the volcano. Ash from the volcano often falls on the houses, shops, offices and factories of the city.

@ **Sakurajima Volcano Research Center**
www.dpri.kyoto-u.ac.jp/~kazan/default_e.html

Landscape

The landscape of China ranges from high mountains and plateaux in the west to lower plains in the east. Its major rivers flow from west to east towards the Pacific Ocean.

Facts about China

Landscape
Area: 9 584 492 sq km
Highest point: Gongga Shan 7514 m

Population
Total: 1 332 079 000
Density: 139 persons per sq km

Settlement
% Urban population: 51
Main towns/cities: Beijing, Shanghai, Wuhan, Guangzhou, Shenzhen

Land use
Main crops: Rice, wheat, potatoes, corn, peanuts
Main industries: Electrical and other machinery, clothing, textiles, iron and steel

Development indicators
Life expectancy: male 72, female 75
GNI per capita: US$ 4940
Primary school enrolment ratio: 99
% Access to safe water: 91

Earthquake zones

China is located in one of the most active seismic regions of the world. In the Tangshan earthquake, in 1976, over 240 000 people lost their lives and more recently, in 2008, 80 000 people were killed during the earthquake in Sichuan Province.

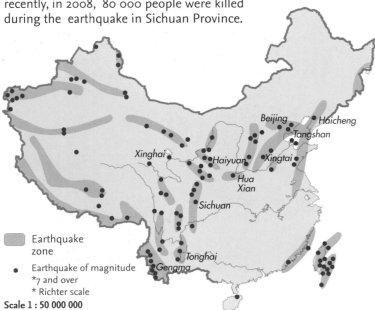

Earthquake zone

• Earthquake of magnitude
*7 and over
* Richter scale

Scale 1 : 50 000 000

Population

China has been the world's most populous nation for many centuries. In the early 1970s, the government implemented a stringent one-child birth-control policy in an attempt to slow down the population growth rate which is now more stable. Life expectancy has risen and China has an increasingly ageing population.

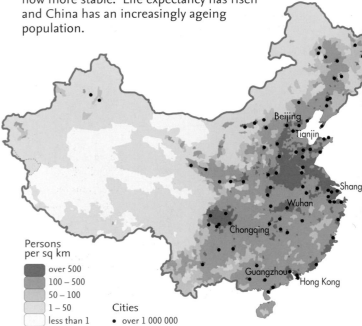

Persons per sq km
■ over 500
■ 100 – 500
■ 50 – 100
□ 1 – 50
□ less than 1
Cities
• over 1 000 000

Scale 1 : 50 000 000

Population change

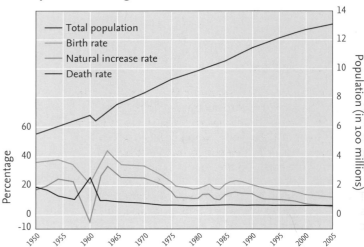

— Total population
— Birth rate
— Natural increase rate
— Death rate

Population structure

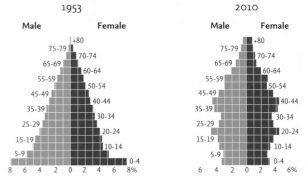

Each full square represents 1% of the total population

Environmental pollution

Rapid industrial development and an increase in energy consumption in China has resulted in serious pollution problems such as smog and degradation of natural resources.

Many of the world's most polluted cities are in China. Acid rain falls on nearly one third of the country.

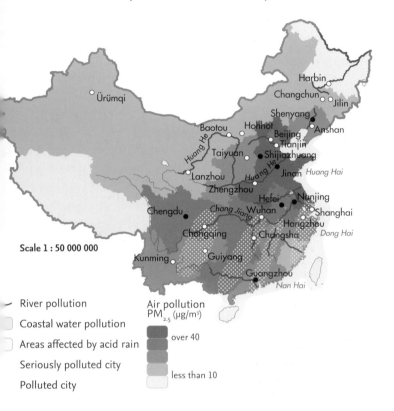

Scale 1 : 50 000 000

- River pollution
- Coastal water pollution
- Areas affected by acid rain
- Seriously polluted city
- Polluted city

Air pollution PM$_{2.5}$ (µg/m³)
- over 40
- less than 10

Soil degradation and desertification

Almost all of China's rivers are polluted to some degree. Overgrazing and the expansion of agricultural land has led to serious desertification in northern China.

Plans to combat these problems include forest planting schemes, pollution control projects and the installation of rubbish treatment plants.

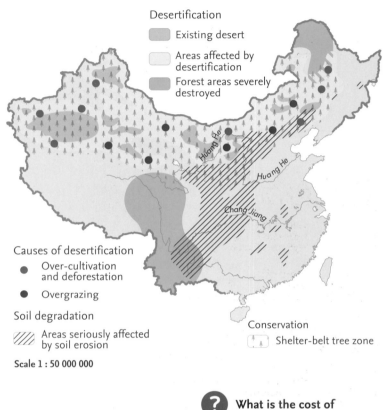

Desertification
- Existing desert
- Areas affected by desertification
- Forest areas severely destroyed

Causes of desertification
- Over-cultivation and deforestation
- Overgrazing

Soil degradation
- Areas seriously affected by soil erosion

Conservation
- Shelter-belt tree zone

Scale 1 : 50 000 000

? **What is the cost of rapid economic growth?**

Three Gorges Dam

The Three Gorges Dam, spanning the Chang Jiang in China, is the largest hydroelectric power project in the world. The dam body was completed in 2006 and the length of the reservoir is 600 kilometres. The project produces clean electricity, prevents deadly floods downstream and improves navigation.

The dam has also flooded archaeological and cultural sites and displaced some 1.24 million people and is causing dramatic ecological changes.

- Area affected by Three Gorges project
- Three Gorges Dam
- Gorge
- Inundated town
- Area inundated
- Provincial boundary

Scale 1 : 4 500 000

Space Imaging

An aerial view of the Three Gorges Dam with the dam clearly visible in the bottom right hand corner.

@ USGS National Earthquake Information Center
www.earthquake.usgs.gov/regional/neic
International Rivers
www.internationalrivers.org
China Population Information and Research Center www.un.org/Depts/escap/pop/china/welcome.htm

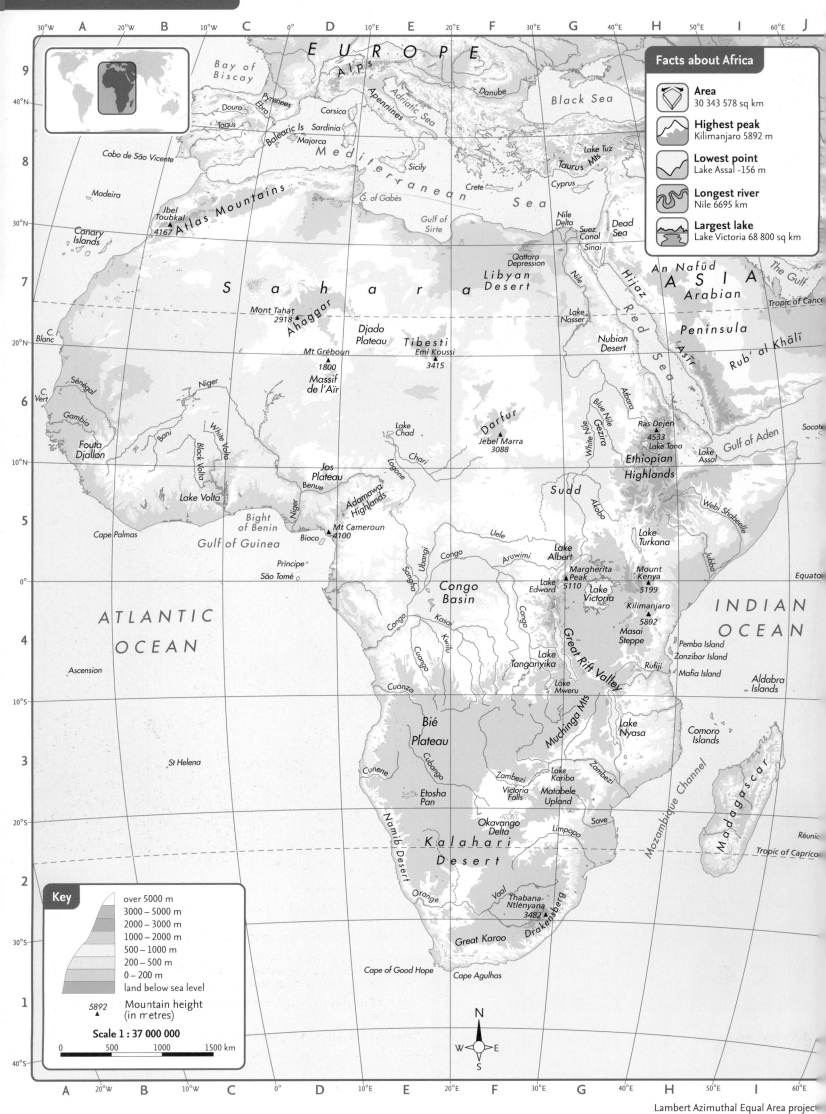

Facts about Africa

Area
30 343 578 sq km

Highest peak
Kilimanjaro 5892 m

Lowest point
Lake Assal -156 m

Longest river
Nile 6695 km

Largest lake
Lake Victoria 68 800 sq km

Key

- over 5000 m
- 3000 – 5000 m
- 2000 – 3000 m
- 1000 – 2000 m
- 500 – 1000 m
- 200 – 500 m
- 0 – 200 m
- land below sea level

5892 ▲ Mountain height (in metres)

Scale 1 : 37 000 000

0   500   1000   1500 km

Lambert Azimuthal Equal Area projection

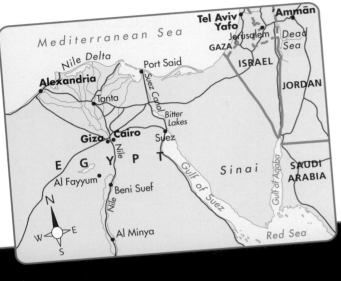

This is an infra-red satellite image of the delta of the river Nile, the Sinai peninsula and the neighbouring parts of Israel, Jordan and Saudi Arabia. Most of this area is desert and this is shown in the pale pinky-brown colour. The red colour in the delta of the river Nile shows that most of the land here is used for farming. The pale blue areas on the edge of the delta are shallow lagoons.

? Connections - Africa and Asia.

@ Visible Earth
visibleearth.nasa.gov

1 The city of Cairo is the dark grey area at the base of the delta.

2 The valley of the river Nile is shown as a dark line which ends at the delta.

3 The Suez Canal was built in 1869 by connecting a series of lakes which are shown in black. The Suez Canal allows ships to sail from the Mediterranean Sea, in the north of the image, to the Red Sea.

4 The Red Sea is shown in black on the image. The pale grey areas in the sea are islands.

5 The Dead Sea in Israel is shown in black on the satellite image.

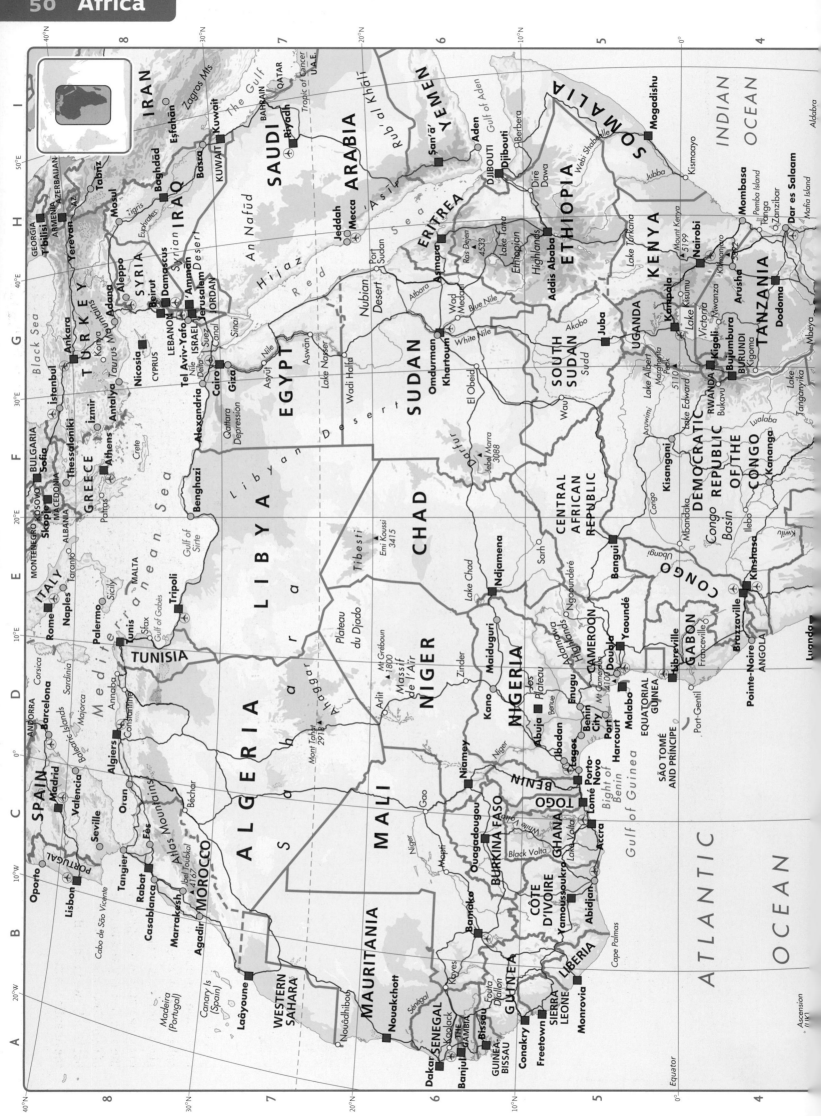

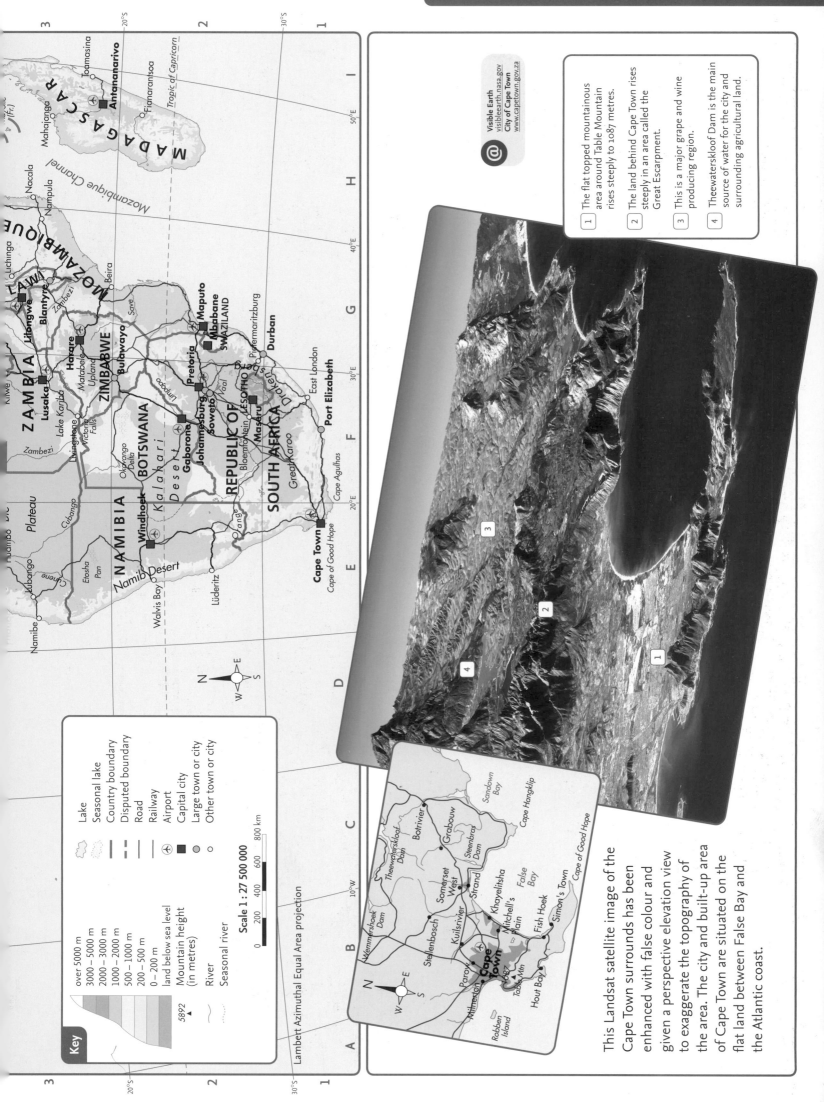

@ Visible Earth
visibleearth.nasa.gov
City of Cape Town
www.capetown.gov.za

1 The flat topped mountainous area around Table Mountain rises steeply to 1087 metres.

2 The land behind Cape Town rises steeply in an area called the Great Escarpment.

3 This is a major grape and wine producing region.

4 Theewaterskloof Dam is the main source of water for the city and surrounding agricultural land.

This Landsat satellite image of the Cape Town surrounds has been enhanced with false colour and given a perspective elevation view to exaggerate the topography of the area. The city and built-up area of Cape Town are situated on the flat land between False Bay and the Atlantic coast.

Key

over 5000 m
3000 – 5000 m
2000 – 3000 m
1000 – 2000 m
500 – 1000 m
200 – 500 m
0 – 200 m
land below sea level

5892 ▲ Mountain height (in metres)

~~~ River

.... Seasonal river

Lake
Seasonal lake

| Country boundary
| Disputed boundary
Road
Railway
⊕ Airport
■ Capital city
● Large town or city
○ Other town or city

Scale 1 : 27 500 000

0 200 400 600 800 km

Lambert Azimuthal Equal Area projection

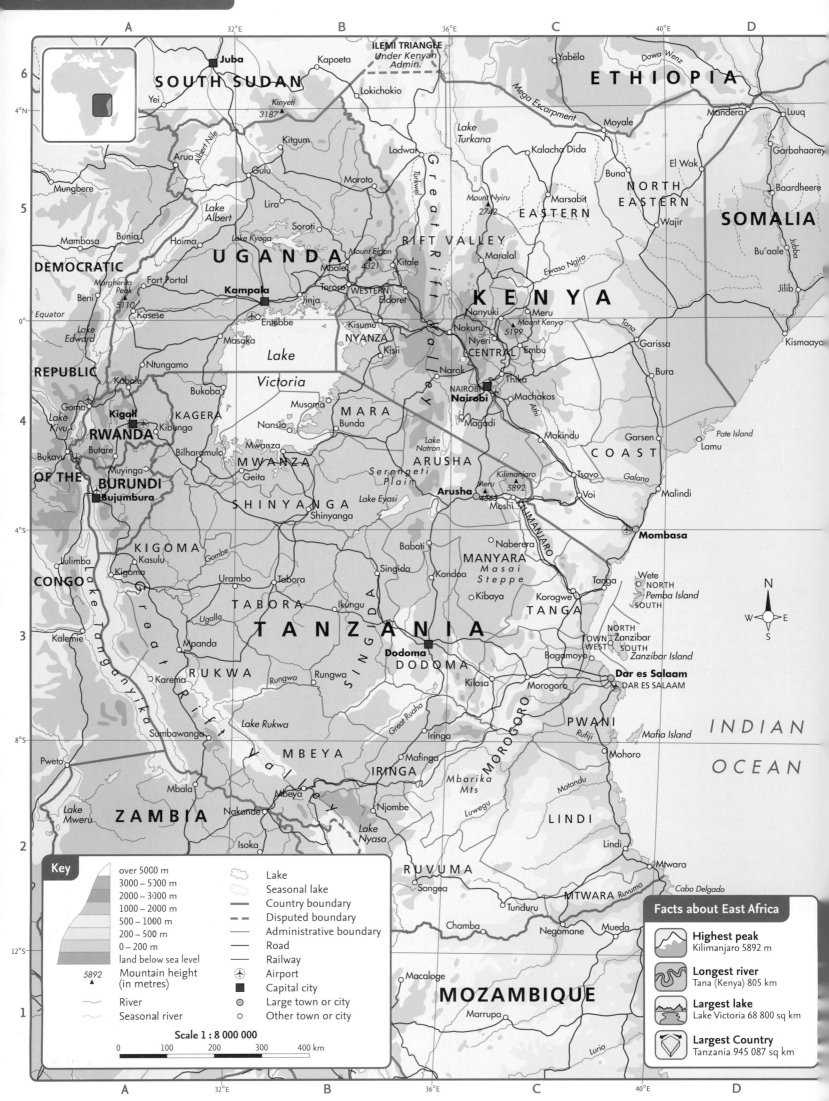

A   32°E   B   36°E   C   40°E   D

SOUTH SUDAN
■ **Juba**
Yei
Kapoeta
ILEMI TRIANGLE
Under Kenyan Admin.
Kinyeti
3187 ▲
Lokichokio
Yabēlo
Dawa Wenz
E T H I O P I A
Mega Escarpment
Moyale
Mandera
Luuq

Kitgum
Arua
Albert Nile
Gulu
Moroto
Lake Turkana
Lodwar
Turkwel
Kalacha Dida
Buna
El Wak
Garbahaarey
Baardheere

Mungbere
Lira
Soroti
Mount Nyiru
2742 ▲
Marsabit
NORTH EASTERN
SOMALIA
Bu'aale

Mambasa
Bunia
Hoima
Lake Kyoga
Mount Elgon
4321 ▲
Kitale
Maralal
Ewaso Ngiro
Wajir
Jilib

DEMOCRATIC
U G A N D A
Fort Portal
Mbale
Tororo
WESTERN
Eldoret
R I F T   V A L L E Y
E A S T E R N

Margherita Peak
5110 ▲
Beni
Kasese
Kampala ■
Jinja
Kisumu
Nanyuki
Meru
Mount Kenya
5199 ▲
K E N Y A

Equator   0°
Lake Edward
Entebbe
NYANZA
Nakuru
Nyeri
CENTRAL
Embu
Tana
Garissa

REPUBLIC
Ntungamo
Masaka
Lake
Kisii
Narok
NAIROBI
Nairobi ■
Thika
Machakos
Bura
Kismaayo

Kabale
Bukoba
Victoria
M A R A
Bunda
Athi
Magadi
Makindu
Garsen
Pate Island
4

Kigali ■
Kibungo
KAGERA
Nansio
Musoma
Lake Natron
ARUSHA
Tsavo
Galana
Lamu

Goma
RWANDA
Butare
Mwanza
MWANZA
Geita
Serengeti Plain
Meru
4565 ▲
Kilimanjaro
5892 ▲
Voi
C O A S T
Malindi

Lake Kivu
Bukavu
Muyinga
Bilharamulo
Lake Eyasi
Arusha
Moshi
Nyumba

OF THE
BURUNDI
SHINYANGA
Shinyanga
KILIMANJARO
4°S

Bujumbura ■
Babati
Naberera
Tanga
Mombasa
Wete
NORTH
Pemba Island
SOUTH

KIGOMA
Kasulu
Gombe
Urambo
Singida
Kondoa
Masai Steppe
Kibaya
Korogwe
TANGA

CONGO
Kigoma
Lake Tanganyika
Great Rift Valley
Tabora
MANYARA
3

Lulimba
Mpanda
Ugalla
Ikungu
S I N G I D A
T A N Z A N I A
Dodoma
DODOMA ■
Kilosa
Morogoro
NORTH Zanzibar **WEST**
SOUTH
Zanzibar Island

Kalemie
TABORA
Rungwa
Rungwa
TOWN WEST
Bagamoyo
Dar es Salaam
■ DAR ES SALAAM

Karema
RUKWA
Great Ruaha
Iringa
Morogoro
PWANI
Mafia Island
I N D I A N

Pweto
Sumbawanga
Lake Rukwa
Mafinga
MBEYA
IRINGA
Rufiji
Mohoro
O C E A N
8°S

Mbala
Mbeya
Iringa
Njombe
Mbarika Mts
Matandu
Luwegu
LINDI

Z A M B I A
Nakonde
Lake Nyasa
Lindi

Lake Mweru
Isoka
RUVUMA
Mtwara
2

Songea
Tunduru
MTWARA
Ruvuma
Cabo Delgado

Chamba
Negomane
Mueda

Macaloge
M O Z A M B I Q U E
Marrupa
Lurio
1

A   32°E   B   36°E   C   40°E   D

Key

| over 5000 m |
| 3000 – 5000 m |
| 2000 – 3000 m |
| 1000 – 2000 m |
| 500 – 1000 m |
| 200 – 500 m |
| 0 – 200 m |
| land below sea level |

5892 ▲ Mountain height (in metres)

~~~ River
······ Seasonal river

⌇ Lake
Seasonal lake
—— Country boundary
- - - Disputed boundary
—— Administrative boundary
—— Road
—— Railway
✈ Airport
■ Capital city
● Large town or city
○ Other town or city

Scale 1 : 8 000 000

0   100   200   300   400 km

Facts about East Africa

Highest peak
Kilimanjaro 5892 m

Longest river
Tana (Kenya) 805 km

Largest lake
Lake Victoria 68 800 sq km

Largest Country
Tanzania 945 087 sq km

Lambert Azimuthal Equal Area project

Annual rainfall

The heaviest rain falls in April and May. The highlands and western areas receive ample rainfall but most of the north and northeast is very dry.

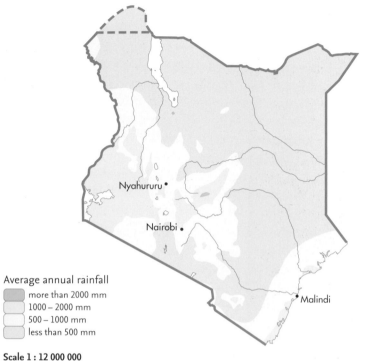

Average annual rainfall
- more than 2000 mm
- 1000 – 2000 mm
- 500 – 1000 mm
- less than 500 mm

Scale 1 : 12 000 000

? **What can we find out about Kenya?**

@ National Bureau of Statistics
www.knbs.or.ke
Met Office Africa Weather
www.metoffice.gov.uk/weather/
africa/africalatest.html

Climate graphs

Kenya has a tropical climate which varies with altitude. The coastal lowland area is hot and humid but the highlands region is much drier and cooler.

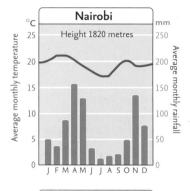

Malindi on the east coast enjoys temperatures around 30 °C all year round. Nyahururu, the highest town in Kenya, and Nairobi have temperatures around 20 °C all year. The wettest month is April in Nairobi and May in Nyahururu and Malindi.

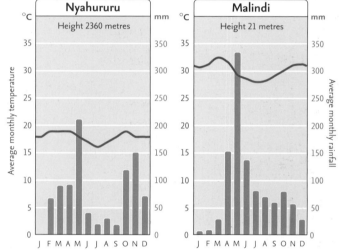

Vegetation

Large areas of Kenya are covered in sparsely wooded Savanna. The most varied vegetation is found in the highlands where Savanna gives way to woodland and forest. North of the river Tana semi desert areas support little vegetation.

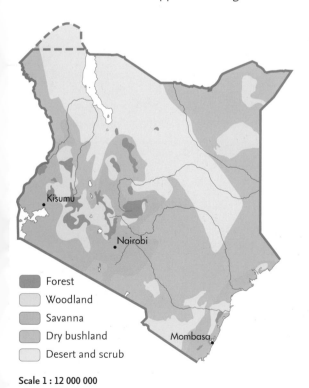

- Forest
- Woodland
- Savanna
- Dry bushland
- Desert and scrub

Scale 1 : 12 000 000

Population

Kenya's population is distributed very unevenly. The most densely populated areas are found in areas with adequate rainfall. The main urban settlements are Nairobi and Mombasa. The dry north and northeast areas are sparsely populated as lack of water limits the development of any settlement.

Central region is more densely populated than Coast region. The population in both regions has grown steadily since 1960.

Persons per sq km
- over 100
- 50 – 100
- 10 – 50
- 1 – 10
- 0 – 1

Cities and towns
- ● over 1 000 000
- ● 100 000 – 1 000 000
- • 25 000 – 100 000

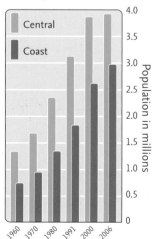

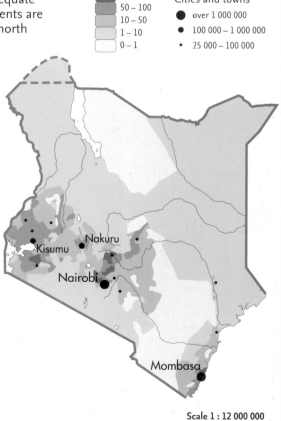

Scale 1 : 12 000 000

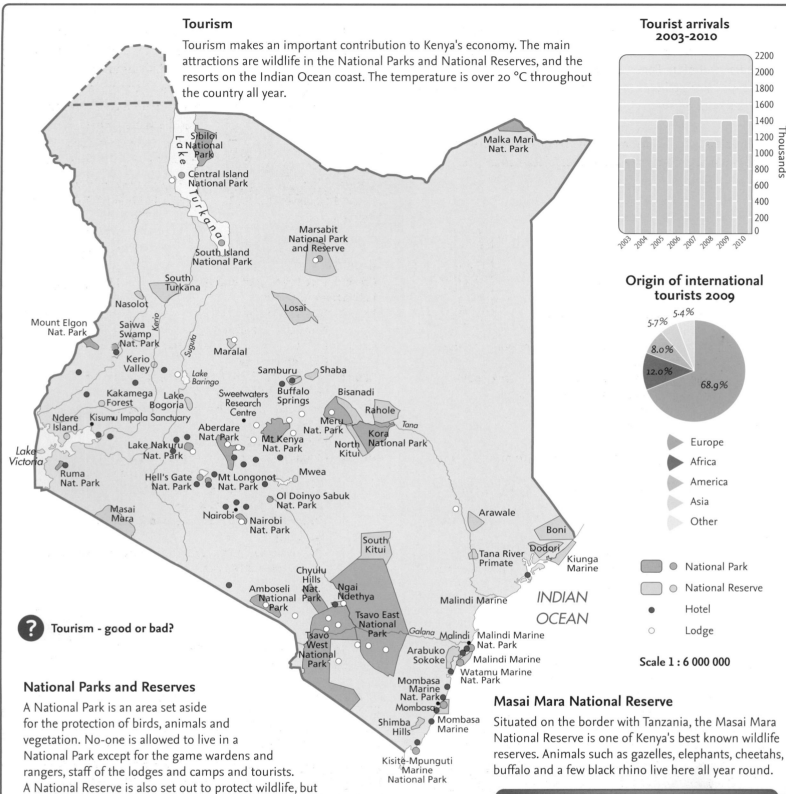

Tourism

Tourism makes an important contribution to Kenya's economy. The main attractions are wildlife in the National Parks and National Reserves, and the resorts on the Indian Ocean coast. The temperature is over 20 °C throughout the country all year.

Tourist arrivals 2003-2010

(Thousands)

2003 2004 2005 2006 2007 2008 2009 2010

Origin of international tourists 2009

- 68.9% Europe
- 12.0% Africa
- 8.0% America
- 5.7% Asia
- 5.4% Other

▷ Europe
▷ Africa
▷ America
▷ Asia
▷ Other

National Park
National Reserve
● Hotel
○ Lodge

Scale 1 : 6 000 000

? Tourism - good or bad?

National Parks and Reserves

A National Park is an area set aside for the protection of birds, animals and vegetation. No-one is allowed to live in a National Park except for the game wardens and rangers, staff of the lodges and camps and tourists. A National Reserve is also set out to protect wildlife, but local people can live and keep their cattle in the reserve.

Endangered species - Rhinos

Since 1980 the Rhino population has declined, due mainly to hunting. Sanctuaries such as the Sweetwaters Research Centre are dedicated to the conservation of the Black Rhino. By 2010 the aim is to increase the population to 650.

Black Rhino population

1980	1987	1993	2003	2005	2007	2010
1500	521	417	428	539	577	630

Kenya Tourist Board
www.magicalkenya.com
The Africa Guide
www.africaguide.com

Masai Mara National Reserve

Situated on the border with Tanzania, the Masai Mara National Reserve is one of Kenya's best known wildlife reserves. Animals such as gazelles, elephants, cheetahs, buffalo and a few black rhino live here all year round.

For four months every year herds of wildebeest from Tanzania graze on the Mara plains. Tall grasses are reduced to stubble before the herds trek south again.

Threats to the natural environment in East Africa include deforestation, soil erosion, desertification, water shortage and water pollution. Forest output has declined due to over exploitation and soil erosion has resulted in the silting of dams and the loss of biodiversity.

The three case studies below outline some of the current environmental problems faced in East African countries.

Maathai Wangari

In the 1970s, the Green Belt Movement founded by Maathai Wangari, focused on the planting of trees and environmental conservation. Over the years 30 million seedling trees have been planted in an effort to protect the environment and the habitats of endangered wildlife.

Kenya
Nanyuki River in Rift Valley Province

Issue The Nanyuki river has become shallow and the water is stagnant and dirty.
Local residents rely on river water for domestic use, livestock and farming.

Causes Large scale removal of forest from the river banks and surrounding hills mainly for fuel.

Effect Evaporation of the river water.

Action **River Management**
- Reforestation is essential.
- Local people need to be encouraged to plant more trees.
- Businesses need to be re-located further from the river to reduce pollution of its waters.
- Irrigation needs to be controlled.

On-going concerns
- There is a lack of alternative sources of fuel.
- Climate change has resulted in a loss of snow and ice on the mountain tops.

Uganda
Co-operative farming of organic cotton in Northern Uganda

Issue Degradation of soils in Northern Uganda.

Cause Mis-management of land and poor farming practices.

Action
- Investment by international organisation in organic cotton farming.
- Introduction of crop rotation to include food crops.
- Use of organic pesticides.

Result
- High yield of organic cotton crops.
- Increase in production of food crops such as millet, maize and beans.
- Re-vitalisation of local economy.
- Northern Uganda is now a hub for cotton growing.
- About 24 000 farmers are now growing organic cotton in Lira District.

Tanzania
Receding icecap of Mount Kilimanjaro

These two images illustrate the changes over time in snow cover at the summit of Mount Kilimanjaro. Ice on the summit has shrunk gradually over the past century. Most scientists forecast that the glaciers of Mount Kilimanjaro will be gone by the year 2020. This could be due to climate change and climatologists are currently studying weather trends and environmental changes.

The loss of Kilimanjaro's permanent icecap will impact on local populations who depend on access to melt water from the ice fields for fresh water during dry seasons and monsoon failures.

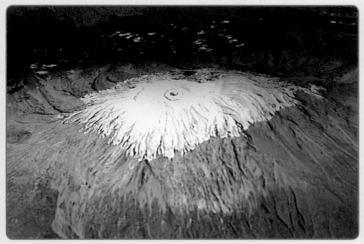

Ice fields on top of Kilimanjaro 1993

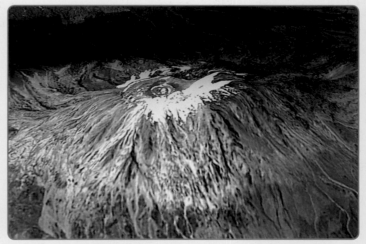

Ice fields on top of Kilimanjaro 2000

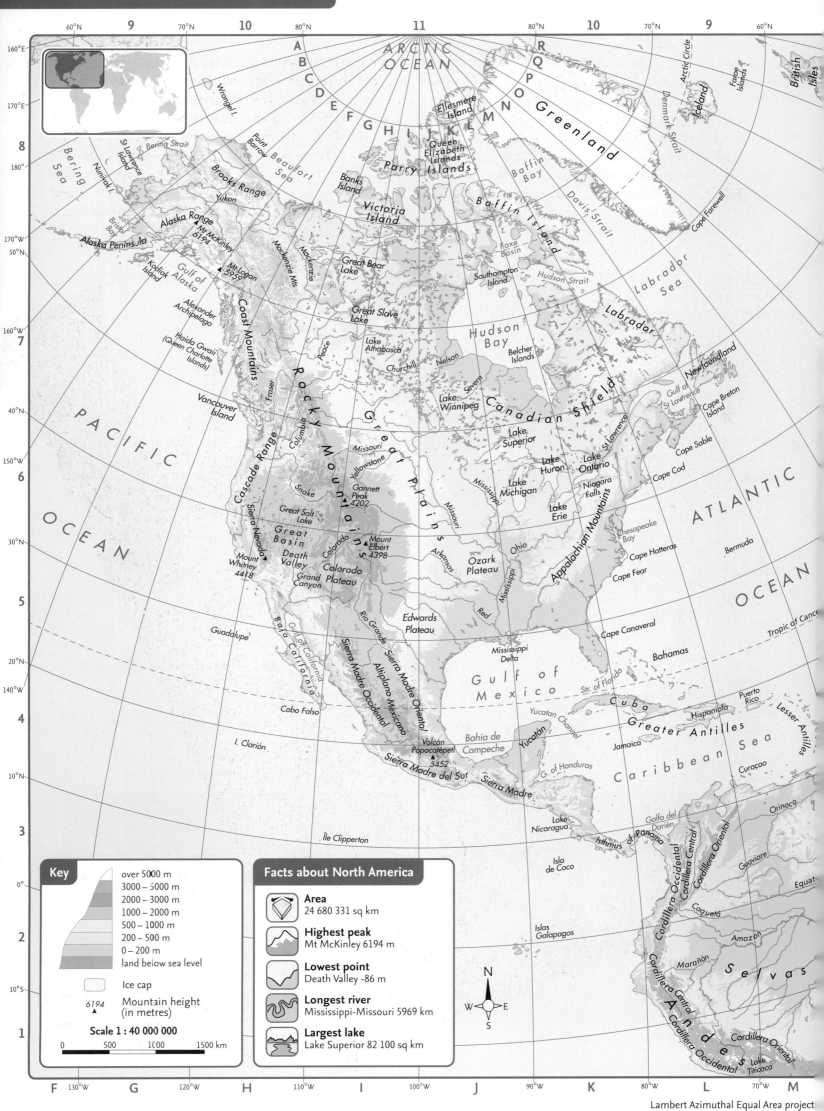

ARCTIC OCEAN

Greenland

Iceland

Faroe Islands

British Isles

Wrangel I.

Point Barrow

Beaufort Sea

Banks Island

Parry Islands

Queen Elizabeth Islands

Ellesmere Island

Denmark Strait

Arctic Circle

Cape Farewell

Bering Sea

St Lawrence Island

Bering Strait

Brooks Range

Yukon

Victoria Island

Baffin Bay

Davis Strait

Labrador Sea

Nunivak I.

Bristol Bay

Alaska Range

Mt McKinley 6194

Great Bear Lake

Southampton Island

Hudson Strait

Labrador

Alaska Penins'la

Gulf of Alaska

Mt Logan 5959

Mackenzie Mts

Mackenzie

Great Slave Lake

Foxe Basin

Newfoundland

Kodiak Island

Alexander Archipelago

Coast Mountains

Peace

Lake Athabasca

Churchill

Nelson

Hudson Bay

Belcher Islands

Gulf of St Lawrence

Cape Breton Island

Haida Gwaii (Queen Charlotte Islands)

Fraser

Severn

Canadian Shield

Vancouver Island

Columbia

Rocky Mountains

Lake Winnipeg

Cascade Range

Missouri

Yellowstone

Great Plains

Lake Superior

Lake Huron

Lake Ontario

St Lawrence

Niagara Falls

Cape Sable

Cape Cod

PACIFIC OCEAN

Snake

Great Salt Lake

Gannett Peak 4202

Mississippi

Lake Michigan

Lake Erie

Appalachian Mountains

ATLANTIC OCEAN

Sierra Nevada

Great Basin

Mount Elbert 4398

Missouri

Ohio

Chesapeake Bay

Cape Hatteras

Bermuda

Mount Whitney 4418

Death Valley

Colorado

Colorado Plateau

Arkansas

Ozark Plateau

Cape Fear

Grand Canyon

Red

Guadalupe

Gulf of California

Baja California

Rio Grande

Edwards Plateau

Mississippi

Cape Canaveral

Tropic of Cancer

Cabo Falso

Sierra Madre Occidental

Sierra Madre Oriental

Mississippi Delta

Gulf of Mexico

Bahamas

Str. of Florida

Cuba

Puerto Rico

Lesser Antilles

I. Clarión

Altiplano Mexicano

Volcán Popocatépetl 5452

Bahía de Campeche

Yucatán

Yucatan Channel

Greater Antilles

Hispaniola

Jamaica

Curaçao

Caribbean Sea

Île Clipperton

Sierra Madre del Sur

Sierra Madre

G. of Honduras

Lake Nicaragua

Golfo del Darién

Isthmus of Panama

Cordillera Occidental

Cordillera Central

Cordillera Oriental

Guaviare

Orinoco

Isla de Coco

Caquetá

Equat

Islas Galapagos

Marañón

Amazon

Cordillera Central

Cordillera Occidental

S e l v a s

A n d e s

Cordillera Oriental

Lake Titicaca

Key

over 5000 m
3000 – 5000 m
2000 – 3000 m
1000 – 2000 m
500 – 1000 m
200 – 500 m
0 – 200 m
land below sea level

Ice cap

6194 Mountain height (in metres)

Scale 1 : 40 000 000

0   500   1000   1500 km

Facts about North America

Area
24 680 331 sq km

Highest peak
Mt McKinley 6194 m

Lowest point
Death Valley -86 m

Longest river
Mississippi-Missouri 5969 km

Largest lake
Lake Superior 82 100 sq km

N
W   E
S

Lambert Azimuthal Equal Area project

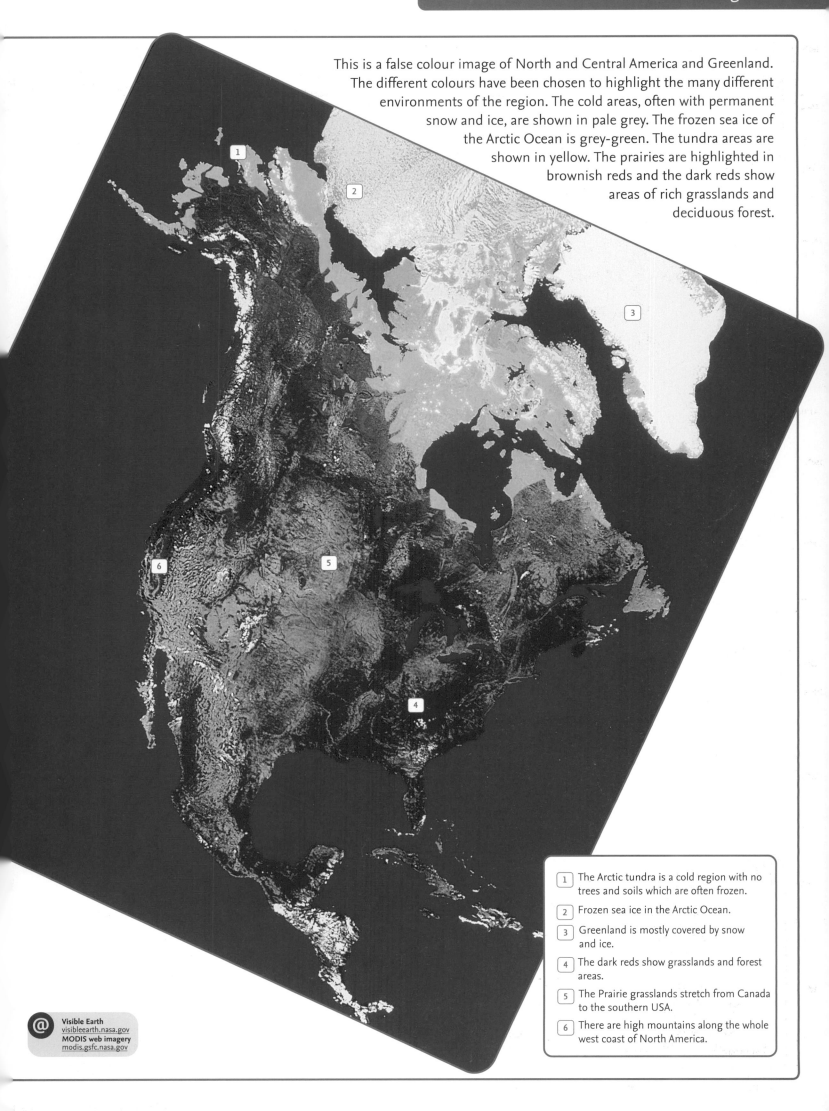

This is a false colour image of North and Central America and Greenland. The different colours have been chosen to highlight the many different environments of the region. The cold areas, often with permanent snow and ice, are shown in pale grey. The frozen sea ice of the Arctic Ocean is grey-green. The tundra areas are shown in yellow. The prairies are highlighted in brownish reds and the dark reds show areas of rich grasslands and deciduous forest.

1 The Arctic tundra is a cold region with no trees and soils which are often frozen.

2 Frozen sea ice in the Arctic Ocean.

3 Greenland is mostly covered by snow and ice.

4 The dark reds show grasslands and forest areas.

5 The Prairie grasslands stretch from Canada to the southern USA.

6 There are high mountains along the whole west coast of North America.

@ **Visible Earth**
visibleearth.nasa.gov
MODIS web imagery
modis.gsfc.nasa.gov

ICELAND
Reykjavik
Arctic Circle
Denmark Strait
GREENLAND (Denmark)
Kong Christian IX Land
Nuuk (Godthåb)
C. Farewell
Davis Strait
Greenland Sea
Baffin Bay
Labrador Sea
Newfoundland St John's
St Pierre and Miquelon (France)
Cape Breton Island
Halifax
Cape Sable
Gulf of St Lawrence
Moncton
Cape Cod
Portland
Boston
Providence
New York
Philadelphia
Baltimore
ATLANTIC

ARCTIC OCEAN
Ellesmere Island
Queen Elizabeth Islands
Prince Patrick Island
Melville Island
Devon Island
Banks Island
Victoria Island
Prince of Wales Island
Parry Islands
Baffin Island
Foxe Basin
Melville Peninsula
Southampton Island
Hudson Strait
Belcher Islands
James Bay
Severn
Canadian Shield
Québec
Montréal
Lake Ontario
Ottawa
Albany
Toronto
Buffalo
Sault Sainte Marie
Lake Huron
Lake Erie
Cleveland
Pittsburgh
Lake Superior
Thunder Bay
Detroit
Lake Michigan
Chicago
Columbus
Milwaukee
Des Moines
Minneapolis-St Paul
Sioux Falls
Omaha
St Joseph
Duluth

Beaufort Sea
Cambridge Bay
Mackenzie
Great Bear Lake
Yellowknife
Hay River
Great Slave Lake
Lake Athabasca
Fort McMurray
Peace
Reindeer Lake
Churchill
Nelson
Churchill
Lake Winnipeg
Lake Manitoba
Winnipeg
Saskatoon
Regina
CANADA
Great Plains
Missouri
UNITED STATES
Wrangel Island
Chukchi Sea
Point Hope
RUSSIAN
Chukotskiy Poluostrov
Anadyr
Anadyrskiy Zaliv
St Lawrence Island
FEDERATION
Bering Strait
Brooks Range
U.S.A. (Alaska)
Fairbanks
Yukon
Alaska Range
Mount McKinley 6194
Anchorage
Seward
Kodiak Island
Bering Sea
Bristol Bay
Alaska Peninsula
Gulf of Alaska
Mackenzie Mountains
Churchill Pk 2819
Rocky Mountains
Mount Logan 5959
Whitehorse
Juneau
Coast Mountains
Alexander Archipelago
Prince Rupert
Haida Gwaii (Queen Charlotte Islands)
Vancouver I.
Mount Waddington 4042
Fraser
Dawson Creek
Grande Prairie
Mt Robson 3954
Edmonton
Calgary
Lethbridge
Yellowstone
Missouri
Garnett Peak 4202
Cheyenne
Denver
Great Salt Lake
Salt Lake City
Mount Elbert 4399
Wheeler Peak 3982
Great Basin
Mount Whitney 4417
Sierra Nevada
Spokane
Snake
Mount Rainier 4392
Vancouver
Victoria
Seattle
Portland
Eugene
Boise
Sacramento
San Francisco
San Jose
Crescent City
Shasta

80° N
70° N
60° N
10° E
0°
10° W
20° W
30° W
40° W
50° W
60° W
70° W
80° W
90° W
170° W
180°
160° W
150° W
140° W
50° N
40° N
60° N
70° N
80° N

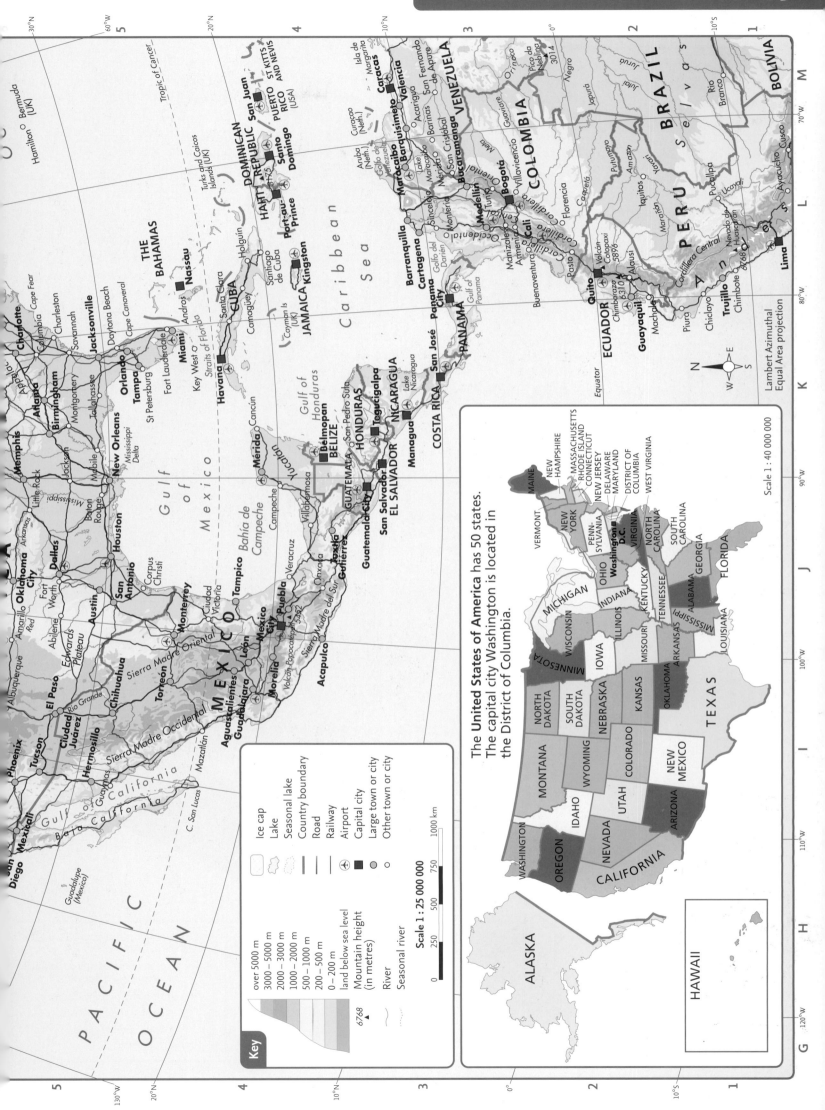

San Francisco

This image of the San Francisco Bay area was photographed from the International Space Station. The grey urban areas contrast with the green hillsides. Pink areas at the southeast of the bay are salt marshes. Tidal channels can be clearly seen within the bay and the outflow of bay water creates a plume as it travels towards the Pacific Ocean.

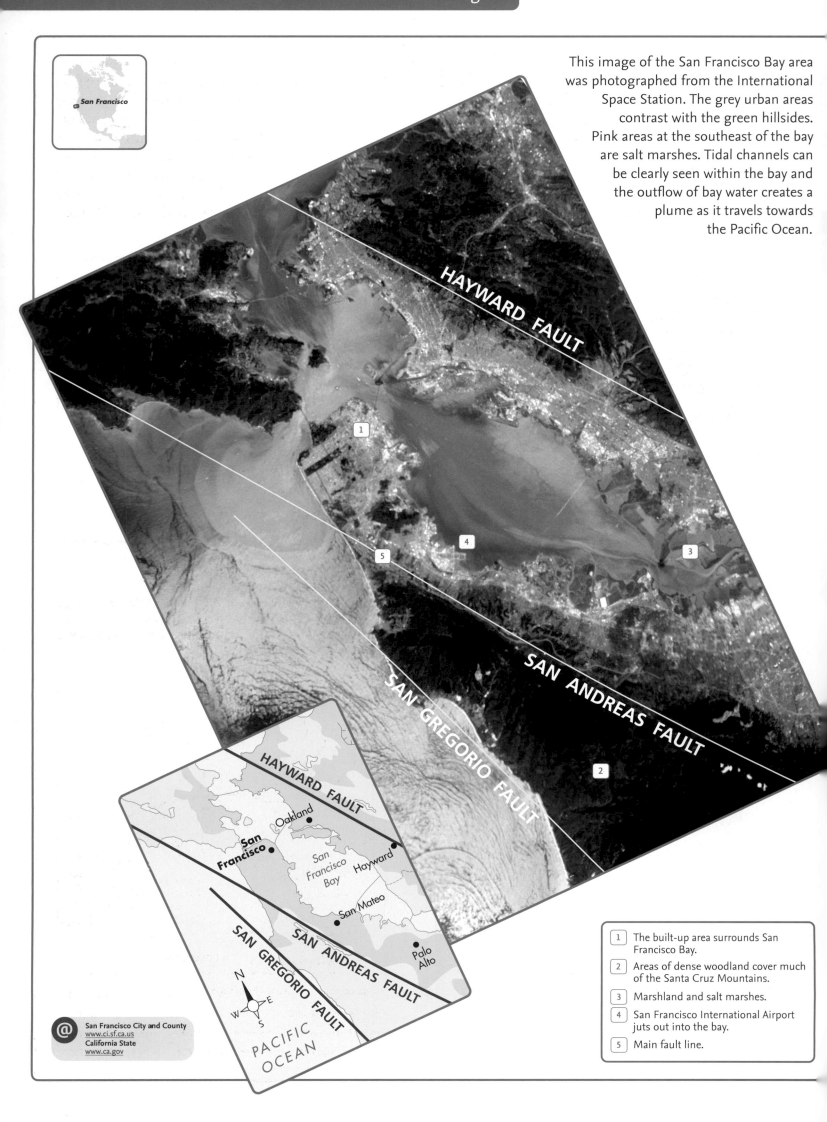

HAYWARD FAULT

SAN ANDREAS FAULT

SAN GREGORIO FAULT

HAYWARD FAULT

Oakland

San Francisco

San Francisco Bay

Hayward

San Mateo

SAN ANDREAS FAULT

Palo Alto

SAN GREGORIO FAULT

N
W   E
S

PACIFIC OCEAN

@ San Francisco City and County
www.ci.sf.ca.us
California State
www.ca.gov

1 The built-up area surrounds San Francisco Bay.

2 Areas of dense woodland cover much of the Santa Cruz Mountains.

3 Marshland and salt marshes.

4 San Francisco International Airport juts out into the bay.

5 Main fault line.

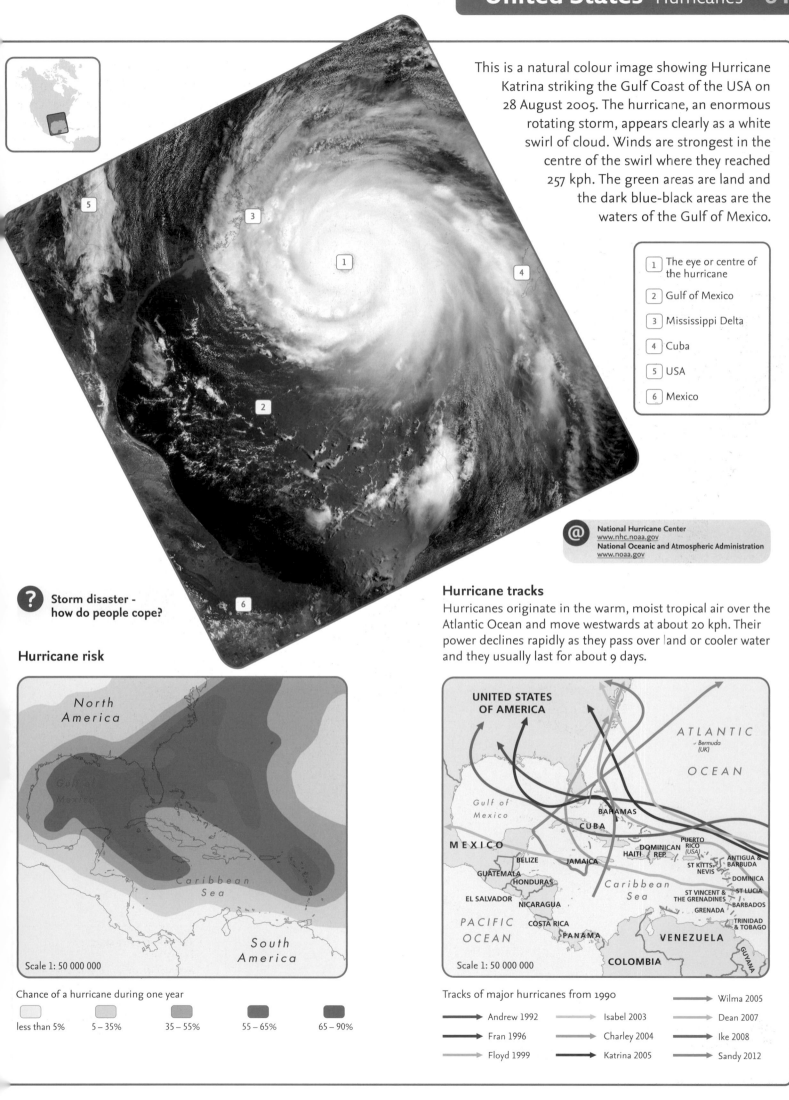

This is a natural colour image showing Hurricane Katrina striking the Gulf Coast of the USA on 28 August 2005. The hurricane, an enormous rotating storm, appears clearly as a white swirl of cloud. Winds are strongest in the centre of the swirl where they reached 257 kph. The green areas are land and the dark blue-black areas are the waters of the Gulf of Mexico.

1 The eye or centre of the hurricane
2 Gulf of Mexico
3 Mississippi Delta
4 Cuba
5 USA
6 Mexico

@ National Hurricane Center
www.nhc.noaa.gov
National Oceanic and Atmospheric Administration
www.noaa.gov

? **Storm disaster - how do people cope?**

Hurricane risk

Hurricane tracks

Hurricanes originate in the warm, moist tropical air over the Atlantic Ocean and move westwards at about 20 kph. Their power declines rapidly as they pass over land or cooler water and they usually last for about 9 days.

North America

Gulf of Mexico

Caribbean Sea

South America

Scale 1: 50 000 000

Chance of a hurricane during one year

less than 5%   5 – 35%   35 – 55%   55 – 65%   65 – 90%

UNITED STATES OF AMERICA

ATLANTIC OCEAN

Bermuda (UK)

Gulf of Mexico

BAHAMAS

CUBA

MEXICO

PUERTO RICO (USA)

DOMINICAN REP.

HAITI

BELIZE   JAMAICA

GUATEMALA

HONDURAS

EL SALVADOR   NICARAGUA

PACIFIC OCEAN   COSTA RICA   PANAMA

ANTIGUA & BARBUDA

ST KITTS NEVIS

DOMINICA

ST LUCIA

ST VINCENT & THE GRENADINES

BARBADOS

GRENADA

TRINIDAD & TOBAGO

Caribbean Sea

VENEZUELA

COLOMBIA

GUYANA

Scale 1: 50 000 000

Tracks of major hurricanes from 1990

→ Andrew 1992   → Isabel 2003   → Wilma 2005
→ Fran 1996   → Charley 2004   → Dean 2007
→ Floyd 1999   → Katrina 2005   → Ike 2008
                              → Sandy 2012

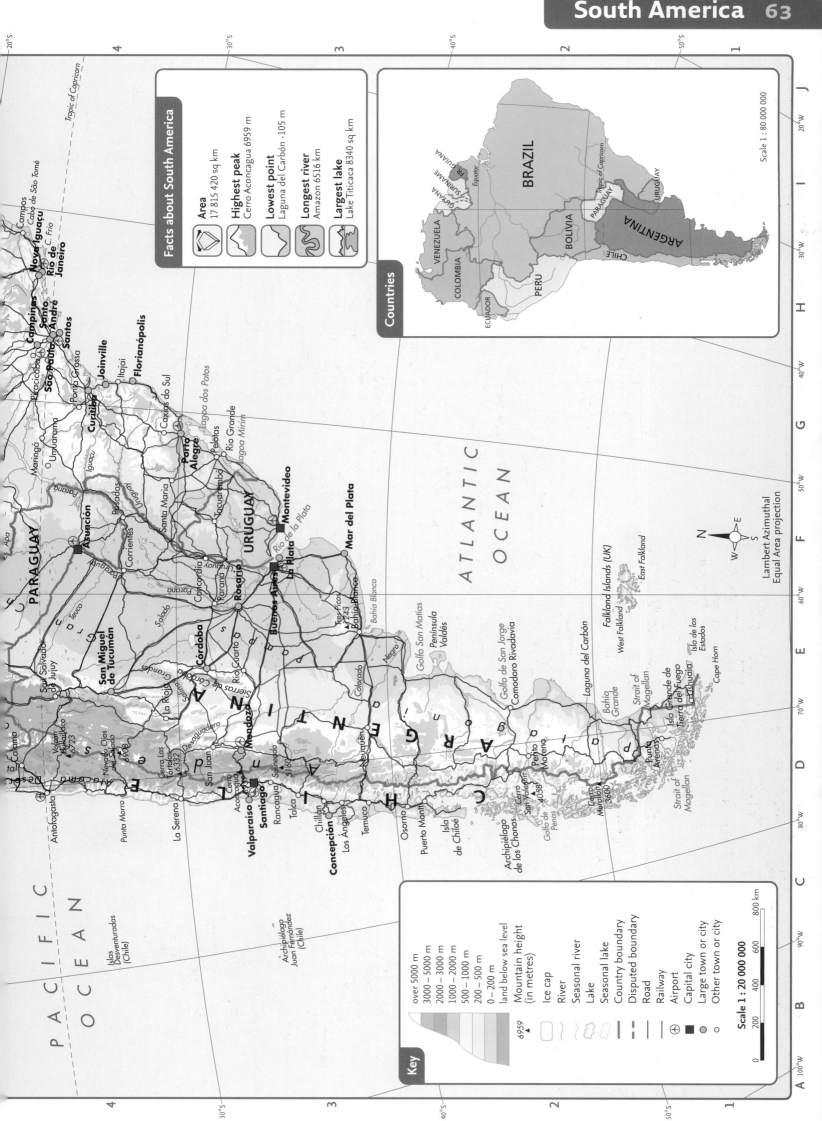

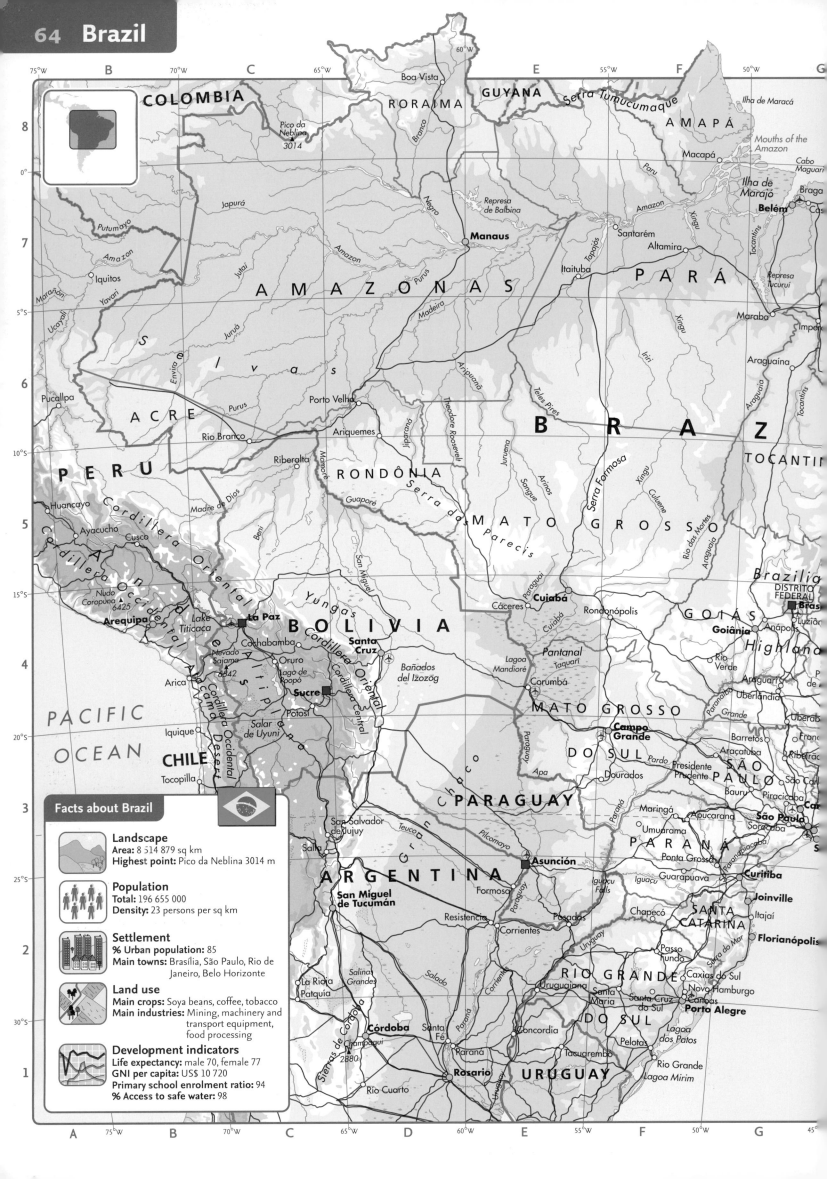

Facts about Brazil

Landscape
Area: 8 514 879 sq km
Highest point: Pico da Neblina 3014 m

Population
Total: 196 655 000
Density: 23 persons per sq km

Settlement
% Urban population: 85
Main towns: Brasília, São Paulo, Rio de Janeiro, Belo Horizonte

Land use
Main crops: Soya beans, coffee, tobacco
Main industries: Mining, machinery and transport equipment, food processing

Development indicators
Life expectancy: male 70, female 77
GNI per capita: US$ 10 720
Primary school enrolment ratio: 94
% Access to safe water: 98

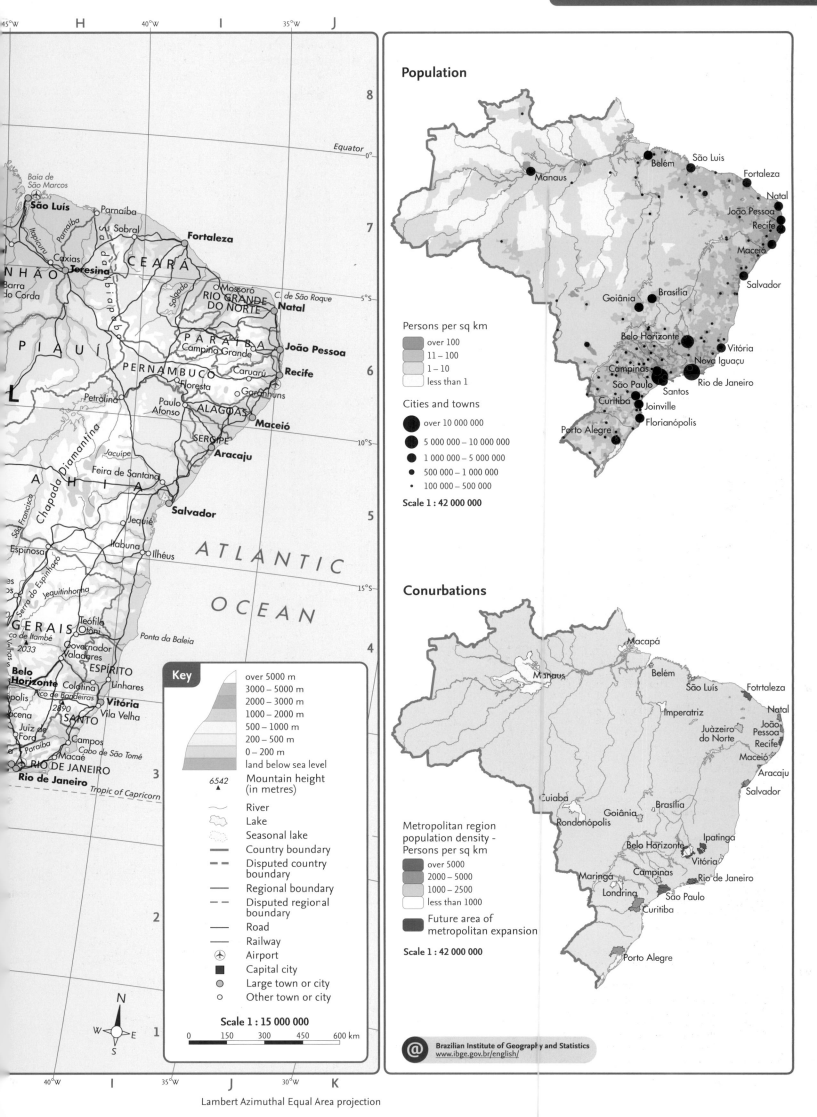

Population

Persons per sq km
- over 100
- 11 – 100
- 1 – 10
- less than 1

Cities and towns
- over 10 000 000
- 5 000 000 – 10 000 000
- 1 000 000 – 5 000 000
- 500 000 – 1 000 000
- 100 000 – 500 000

Scale 1 : 42 000 000

Manaus
Belém
São Luís
Fortaleza
Natal
João Pessoa
Recife
Maceió
Salvador
Goiânia
Brasília
Belo Horizonte
Vitória
Nova Iguaçu
Campinas
São Paulo
Santos
Rio de Janeiro
Curitiba
Joinville
Florianópolis
Porto Alegre

Conurbations

Metropolitan region population density - Persons per sq km
- over 5000
- 2000 – 5000
- 1000 – 2500
- less than 1000
- Future area of metropolitan expansion

Scale 1 : 42 000 000

Macapá
Manaus
Belém
São Luís
Fotrtaleza
Natal
Imperatriz
Juàzeiro do Norte
João Pessoa
Recife
Maceió
Aracaju
Salvador
Cuiabá
Brasília
Goiânia
Rondonópolis
Belo Horizonte
Ipatinga
Vitória
Maringá
Campinas
Rio de Janeiro
Londrina
São Paulo
Curitiba
Porto Alegre

@ **Brazilian Institute of Geography and Statistics**
www.ibge.gov.br/english/

Key

| over 5000 m |
| 3000 – 5000 m |
| 2000 – 3000 m |
| 1000 – 2000 m |
| 500 – 1000 m |
| 200 – 500 m |
| 0 – 200 m |
| land below sea level |

6542 ▲ Mountain height (in metres)

River
Lake
Seasonal lake
Country boundary
Disputed country boundary
Regional boundary
Disputed regional boundary
Road
Railway
✈ Airport
■ Capital city
◉ Large town or city
○ Other town or city

Scale 1 : 15 000 000

0   150   300   450   600 km

N W E S

Map labels (main map)

45°W   H   40°W   I   35°W   J
Equator   0°

Baía de São Marcos
São Luís
Parnaíba
Itapicuru
Parnaíba
Sobral
Fortaleza
Caxias
Teresina
CEARÁ
Barra do Corda
NHÃO
Mossoró
C. de São Roque
5°S
Salgado
RIO GRANDE DO NORTE
Natal
PIAUÍ
PARAÍBA
Campina Grande
João Pessoa
PERNAMBUCO
Caruarú
Recife
Floresta
Garanhuns
Petrolina
Paulo Afonso
ALAGOAS
Maceió
SERGIPE
Aracaju
10°S
Chapada Diamantina
Jacuípe
Feira de Santana
São Francisco
BAHIA
Salvador
Jequié
Itabuna
Espinosa
Ilhéus
ATLANTIC
15°S
Serra do Espinhaço
Jequitinhonha
OCEAN
Ponta da Baleia
GERAIS
Teófilo Otôni
Pico de Itambé
2033
Governador Valadares
ESPÍRITO
Linhares
Belo Horizonte
Colatina
Vitória
Pico de Bandeiras
2890
SANTO
Vila Velha
Juiz de Fora
Campos
Paraíba
Cabo de São Tomé
Macaé
RIO DE JANEIRO
Rio de Janeiro
Tropic of Capricorn

8
7
6
5
4
3
2
1

ATLANTIC OCEAN

40°W   I   35°W   J   30°W   K

Annual rainfall

Average annual rainfall

- more than 2400 mm
- 2000 – 2400 mm
- 1600 – 2000 mm
- 1200 – 1600 mm
- 800 – 1200 mm
- less than 800 mm

Scale 1 : 60 000 000

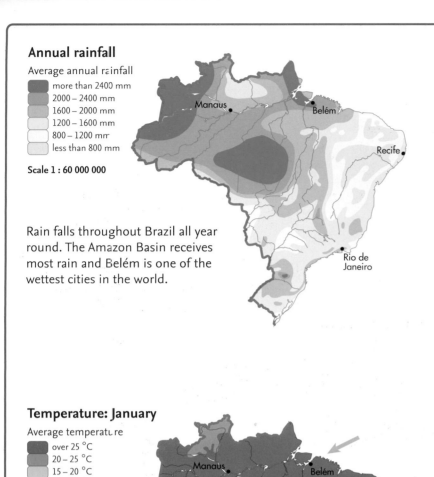

Rain falls throughout Brazil all year round. The Amazon Basin receives most rain and Belém is one of the wettest cities in the world.

Climate graphs

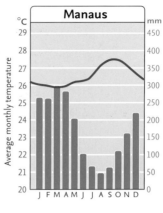

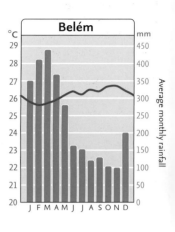

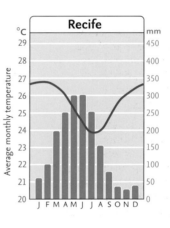

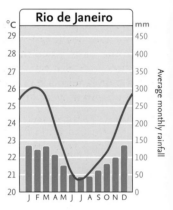

Temperature: January

Average temperature

- over 25 °C
- 20 – 25 °C
- 15 – 20 °C
- 10 – 15 °C
- → Wind direction

Scale 1 : 60 000 000

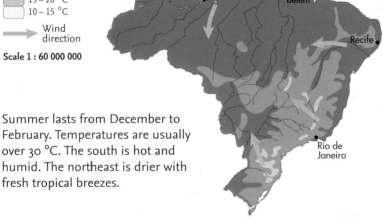

Summer lasts from December to February. Temperatures are usually over 30 °C. The south is hot and humid. The northeast is drier with fresh tropical breezes.

@ **Met Office South America Weather**
www.metoffice.gov.uk/weather/samerica/samericaforecast.html
World Meteorological Organization
www.wmo.ch

Temperature: July

Average temperature

- over 25 °C
- 20 – 25 °C
- 15 – 20 °C
- 10 – 15 °C
- → Wind direction

Scale 1 : 60 000 000

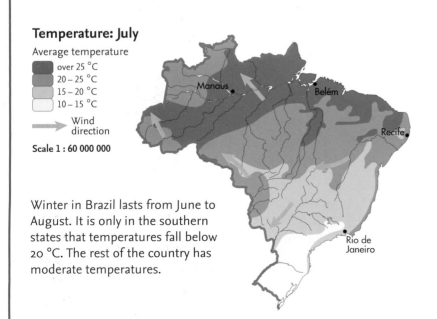

Winter in Brazil lasts from June to August. It is only in the southern states that temperatures fall below 20 °C. The rest of the country has moderate temperatures.

Climate zones

- Equatorial
- Tropical (Equatorial)
- Tropical (Northeast)
- Tropical (Central)
- Temperate

Scale 1 : 60 000 000

Internal Migration

Number of migrants
- over 150 000 people
- 100 000 – 150 000 people
- 20 000 – 100 000 people

Origin of migration by region
- North
- Northeast
- Southeast
- South
- Centre-West

Scale 1 : 28 000 000

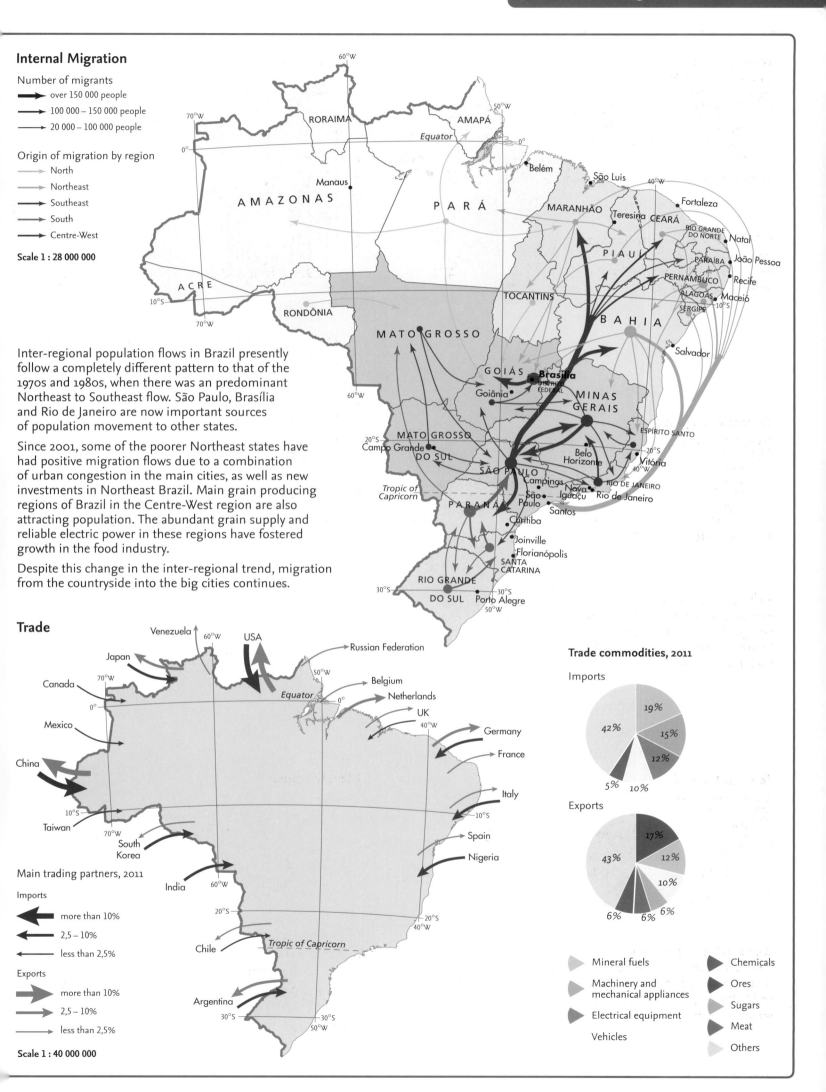

Inter-regional population flows in Brazil presently follow a completely different pattern to that of the 1970s and 1980s, when there was an predominant Northeast to Southeast flow. São Paulo, Brasília and Rio de Janeiro are now important sources of population movement to other states.

Since 2001, some of the poorer Northeast states have had positive migration flows due to a combination of urban congestion in the main cities, as well as new investments in Northeast Brazil. Main grain producing regions of Brazil in the Centre-West region are also attracting population. The abundant grain supply and reliable electric power in these regions have fostered growth in the food industry.

Despite this change in the inter-regional trend, migration from the countryside into the big cities continues.

Trade

Main trading partners, 2011

Imports
- more than 10%
- 2,5 – 10%
- less than 2,5%

Exports
- more than 10%
- 2,5 – 10%
- less than 2,5%

Scale 1 : 40 000 000

Trade commodities, 2011

Imports
- 19%
- 15%
- 12%
- 10%
- 5%
- 42%

Exports
- 17%
- 12%
- 10%
- 6%
- 6%
- 6%
- 43%

- Mineral fuels
- Machinery and mechanical appliances
- Electrical equipment
- Vehicles
- Chemicals
- Ores
- Sugars
- Meat
- Others

This is a true colour image of part of the Amazon rainforest. The Madeira river is a tributary of the Amazon and flows across the top left of the image. The straight lines in the forest show where whole blocks of trees have been cut down. Smoke plumes from forest fires is evidence that slash and burn farming is still being practised in the forest.

1 Areas where the rainforest has not yet been cut down.

2 Deforested areas of land cleared for commercial logging.

3 Smoke plumes from forest fires.

4 Madeira river flowing through the forest.

Amazonia : Development

The largest tropical rainforest in the world is in Amazonia in Brazil. Most deforestation has taken place on the edges of the forest in the east, south and southwest. Satellite images like the one opposite allow the Brazilian government to monitor damage to the forest and take steps to prevent unnecessary exploitation of the forest.

☐ Location of satellite image shown on page 68

HEP developments
▬ HEP Dam
▭ HEP Dam (planned)

Communications
—— Railway
----- Railway (planned)
—— Road
----- Road (planned)

Land Use
⬜ Cropland and woodland
⬜ Grassland and grazing
⬛ Grassland and woodland
⬜ Tropical forest
⬜ Temperate forest
⬜ Scrubland or desert
⬜ Swamp or marsh
⬜ Deforestation
—— Extent of Amazonia in Brazil

Scale 1 : 30 000 000

❓ **Development or destruction?**

Rainforest clearance takes place to make way for industry.

Brazil : Resources

Brazil has a wide variety of mineral resources. It produces high grade manganese and iron ore which are its main exports. Industry is concentrated around the main cities where over 85% of the population live.

Minerals and fuel
■ Iron ore
■ Tin
● Manganese
✕ Bauxite
● Gold
◆ Diamonds
▲ Lead and Zinc
◆ Copper
■ Chromium
◆ Nickel
⬬ Coalfield
⬬ Oilfield and oilsand
⬬ Gasfield
—— Oil pipeline
—— Gas pipeline

Industry
▨ Iron / Steel
▥ Oil refineries
▣ Shipbuilding
✈ Aircraft
✳ Mechanical engineering
▣ Electronics
▨ Publishing / Paper
▨ Chemicals
▨ Textiles / Clothing
▣ Food processing
• Major industrial centre

Scale 1 : 30 000 000

@ **Brazilian Institute of Geography and Statistics**
www.ibge.gov.br/english/

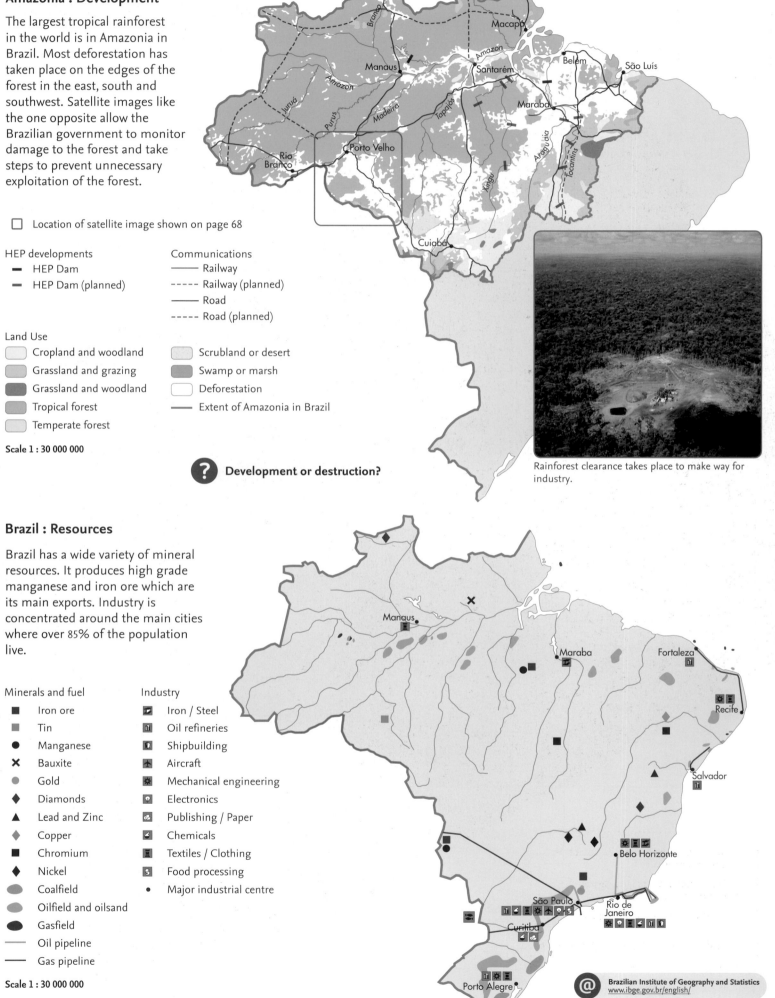

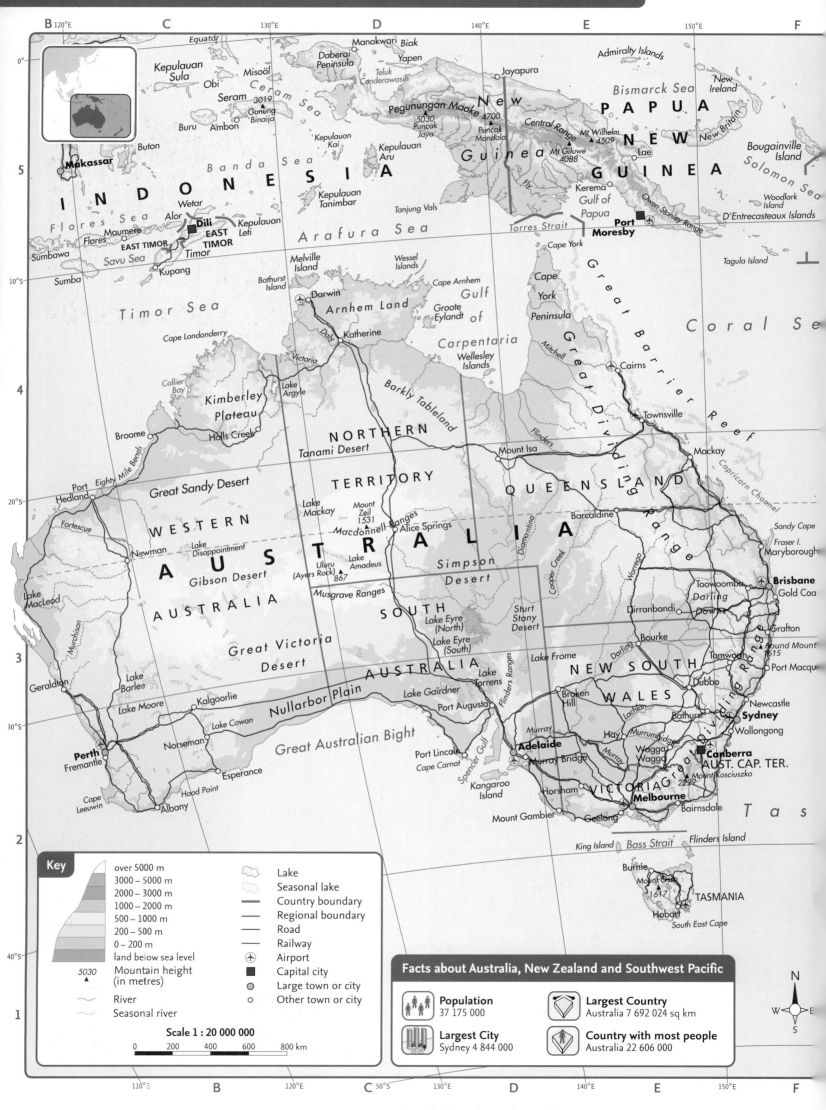

Key

over 5000 m	
3000 – 5000 m	
2000 – 3000 m	
1000 – 2000 m	
500 – 1000 m	
200 – 500 m	
0 – 200 m	
land below sea level	

5030 ▲ Mountain height (in metres)

〰 River
⋯ Seasonal river

Lake
Seasonal lake
Country boundary
Regional boundary
Road
Railway
✈ Airport
■ Capital city
● Large town or city
○ Other town or city

Scale 1 : 20 000 000

0   200   400   600   800 km

Facts about Australia, New Zealand and Southwest Pacific

Population
37 175 000

Largest Country
Australia 7 692 024 sq km

Largest City
Sydney 4 844 000

Country with most people
Australia 22 606 000

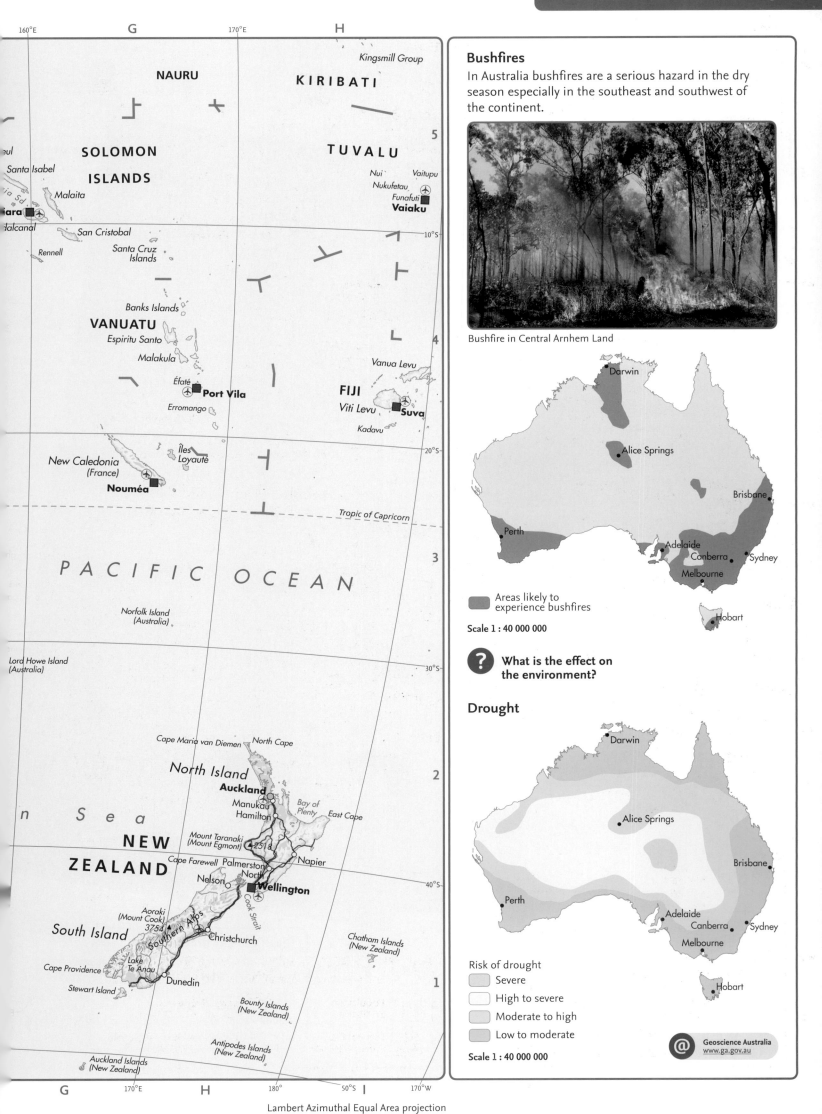

Bushfires

In Australia bushfires are a serious hazard in the dry season especially in the southeast and southwest of the continent.

Bushfire in Central Arnhem Land

Areas likely to experience bushfires

Scale 1 : 40 000 000

? **What is the effect on the environment?**

Drought

Risk of drought
- Severe
- High to severe
- Moderate to high
- Low to moderate

Scale 1 : 40 000 000

@ Geoscience Australia
www.ga.gov.au

Lambert Azimuthal Equal Area projection

This is a simulated natural colour image of Australia, New Zealand and the nearby parts of southeast Asia and the southwest Pacific Ocean. The desert of central and western Australia is shown in pink-brown, whilst the greens on the image show those areas with forests and farmland. Areas of grassland are shown in grey-green.

@ **Visible Earth**
visibleearth.nasa.gov
MODIS web imagery
modis.gsfc.nasa.gov

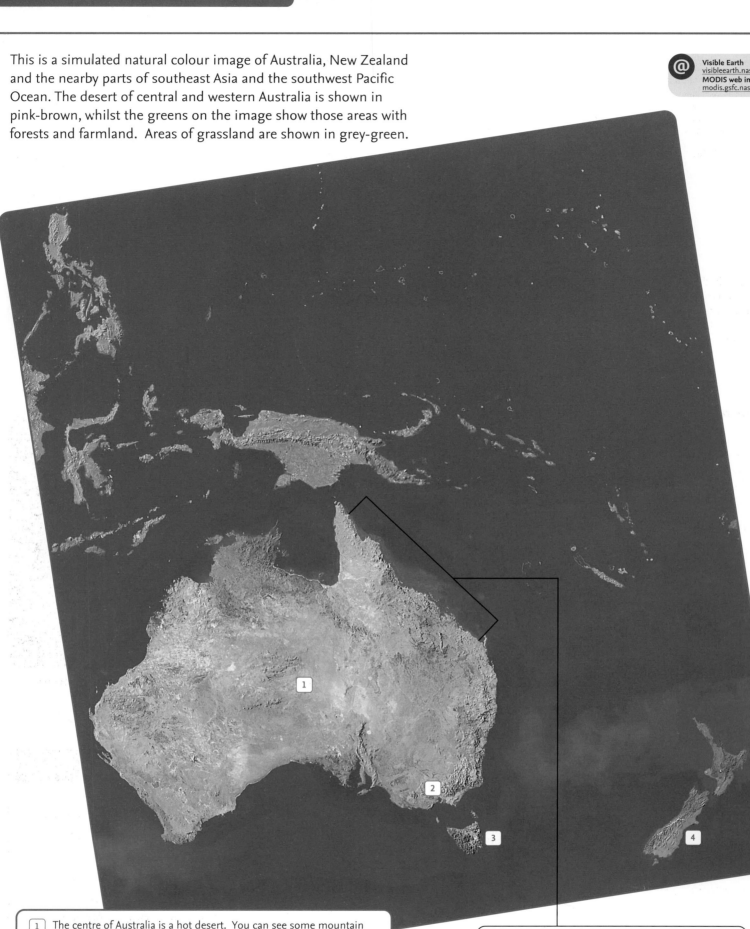

1 The centre of Australia is a hot desert. You can see some mountain ranges in the western areas.

2 Southeast Australia is one of the main farming areas of the country as the green colours show.

3 The island of Tasmania is covered by grassland, forest and farmland.

4 Because New Zealand is further south than Australia it is cooler and wetter. As a result there are more forests.

Fragile Environment
The Great Barrier Reef, along the Queensland coast, is the largest barrier reef in the world. The impact of over-fishing, pollution, coral bleaching and sea temperatures rises due to global warming requires action to protect and preserve this unique environment.

Annual rainfall

Average annual rainfall
- 1000 – 2000 mm
- 500 – 1000 mm
- 250 – 500 mm
- less than 250 mm

Scale 1 : 60 000 000

Australia is the driest continent and rainfall is highly variable across the country. The wettest areas are northeast Queensland and southwest Tasmania; the centre of Australia is hot and dry.

Population

Persons per sq km
- over 50
- 10 – 50
- 1 – 10
- 0 – 1

Cities and towns
- ● 2 500 000 – 5 000 000
- • 1 000 000 – 2 500 000

Scale 1 : 60 000 000

Australia has one of the lowest population densities in the world. Distribution is uneven with most people living along the eastern and south eastern coasts. The main urban areas are Adelaide, Brisbane, Melbourne, Perth and Sydney.

Temperature: January

Average temperature
- over 32 °C
- 24 – 32 °C
- 16 – 24 °C
- 8 – 16 °C

→ Wind direction

Scale 1 : 60 000 000

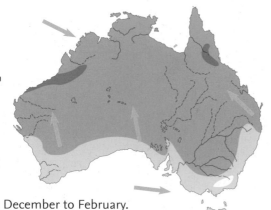

Summer lasts from December to February. In January average temperatures exceed 30 °C. The hottest areas are northwest Western Australia and from southwest Queensland across south Australia into southeast Western Australia.

@ World Meteorological Organization www.wmo.ch
Met Office Australia Weather www.metoffice.gov.uk/weather/australasia/australasiaforecast.html
Australian Bureau of Statistics www.abs.gov.au

? Where are the people?

Sydney Space Imaging

Sydney is Australia's largest city with a population of 4 844 000.

Temperature: July

Average temperature
- over 24 °C
- 16 – 24 °C
- 8 – 16 °C
- 0 – 8 °C
- below 0 °C

→ Wind direction

Scale 1 : 60 000 000

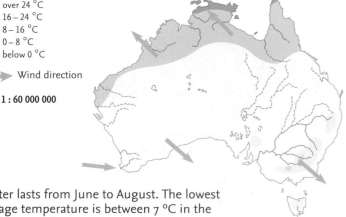

Winter lasts from June to August. The lowest average temperature is between 7 °C in the northwest and 5 °C in the southeast. Snow is confined to the mountainous regions of the southeast.

Facts about Australia

Landscape
Area: 7 692 024 sq km
Highest point: Mount Kosciuszko 2229 m

Population
Total: 22 606 000
Density: 3 persons per sq km

Settlement
% Urban population: 89
Main towns/cities: Sydney, Melbourne, Adelaide, Brisbane, Perth

Land use
Main crops: Wheat, sugar, rice, barley
Main industries: Food products, chemicals, transport equipment

Development indicators
Life expectancy: male 80, female 84
GNI per capita: US$ 46 200
Primary school enrolment ratio: 97
% Access to safe water: 100

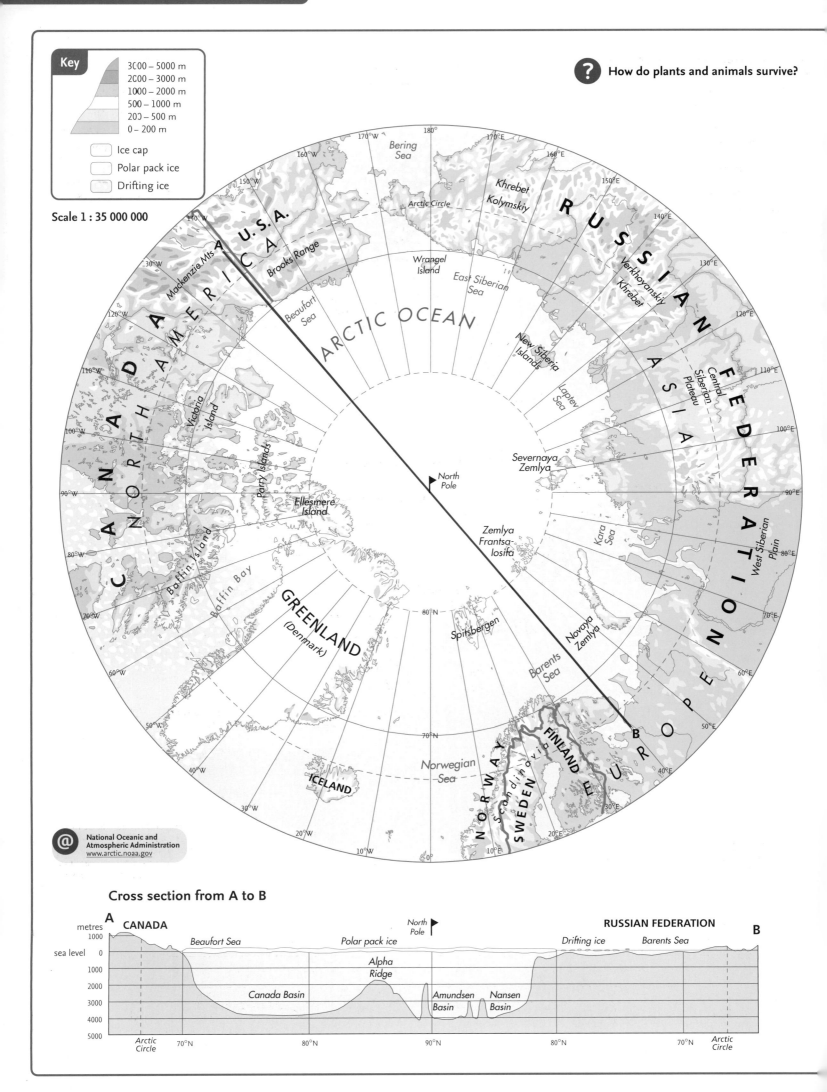

Key

3000 – 5000 m	
2000 – 3000 m	
1000 – 2000 m	
500 – 1000 m	
200 – 500 m	
0 – 200 m	

Ice cap
Polar pack ice
Drifting ice

Scale 1 : 35 000 000

? How do plants and animals survive?

National Oceanic and
Atmospheric Administration
www.arctic.noaa.gov

Cross section from A to B

A CANADA

North Pole

RUSSIAN FEDERATION   B

metres
1000
sea level 0
1000
2000
3000
4000
5000

Beaufort Sea
Polar pack ice
Drifting ice
Barents Sea

Alpha Ridge
Canada Basin
Amundsen Basin
Nansen Basin

Arctic Circle   70°N   80°N   90°N   80°N   70°N   Arctic Circle

Polar Stereographic project

Manned bases in the Antarctic Peninsula

1. Frei (Chile)
2. Comandante Ferraz (Brazil)
3. Bellingshausen (Russian Federation)
4. Jubany (Argentina)
5. Arctowski (Poland)
6. O'Higgins (Chile)
7. Great Wall (China)
8. Artigas (Uruguay)
9. Escudero (Chile)
10. San Martin (Argentina)
11. Arturo Prat (Chile)
12. Estación Marítima Antártica (Chile)

? Why is Antarctica a fragile environment?

Orcadas (Arg.)
South Orkney Is.

SANAE IV (South Africa)
Neumayer III (Germany)
Maitri (India)
Novolazarevskaya (Rus. Fed.)
Syowa (Japan)
Antarctic Circle
Troll (Norway)
Princess Elisabeth (Belgium)
Queen Maud Land
Enderby Land
SOUTHERN

South Shetland Is.
King Sejong (Korea)
Esperanza (Arg.)
Marambio (Arg.)
Halley (UK)
Weddell Sea
Mawson (Australia)
Kemp Land

Palmer (USA)
Vernadskiy (Ukraine)
Rothera (UK)
Antarctic Peninsula
Graham Land
Palmer Land
Alexander I.
Belgrano II (Arg.)
Berkner I.
Prydz Bay
Progress (Rus. Fed.)
Davis (Australia)
Zhongshan (China)

SOUTHERN OCEAN
Bellingshausen Sea
Ellsworth Land
A
ANTARCTICA
South Pole
Amundsen-Scott (USA)
Mirnyy (Rus. Fed.)
Queen Mary Land
B
OCEAN

Amundsen Sea
Mary Byrd Land
Vostok (Rus. Fed.)
Concordia (France/Italy)
Casey (Australia)

Ross Ice Shelf
Roosevelt I.
McMurdo (USA)
Scott Base (NZ)
Wilkes Land

Ross Sea
Oates Land
Dumont d'Urville (France)

@ British Antarctic Survey
www.antarctica.ac.uk
Council of Managers of National Antarctic Program
www.comnap.aq

Under the Antarctic Treaty of 1959 all territorial claims are held in abeyance in the interest of international co-operation for scientific purposes.

Cross section from A to B

Bellingshausen Sea
metres
A
Western ice sheet
Transantarctic Mountains
Eastern ice sheet
B
3000
2000
1000
sea level 0
1000
2000
80°S
80°S
70°S
Antarctic Circle

Polar Stereographic projection

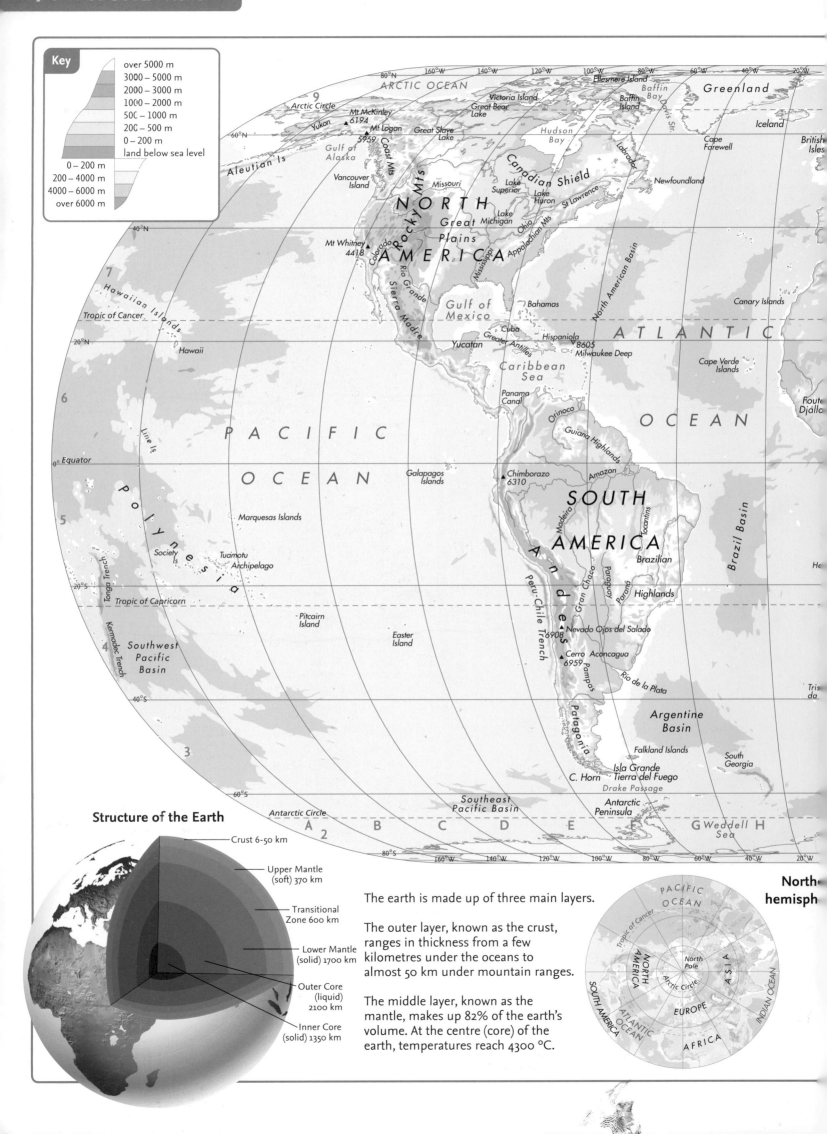

Key

- over 5000 m
- 3000 – 5000 m
- 2000 – 3000 m
- 1000 – 2000 m
- 500 – 1000 m
- 200 – 500 m
- 0 – 200 m
- land below sea level

- 0 – 200 m
- 200 – 4000 m
- 4000 – 6000 m
- over 6000 m

ARCTIC OCEAN

80°N 160°W 140°W 120°W 100°W 80°W 60°W 40°W 20°W

Ellesmere Island
Baffin Bay
Greenland

Arctic Circle
Victoria Island
Great Bear Lake
Baffin Island
Davis Str.

Iceland

60°N
Yukon
Mt McKinley 6194
Mt Logan 5959
Great Slave Lake
Hudson Bay
Labrador
Cape Farewell

British Isles

Aleutian Is
Gulf of Alaska
Coast Mts
Newfoundland

Vancouver Island
NORTH
Canadian Shield
Lake Superior
Lake Huron
St Lawrence

40°N
Rocky Mts
Great Plains
AMERICA
Lake Michigan
Ohio
Appalachian Mts
North American Basin

Mt Whitney 4418
Colorado
Missouri
Mississippi

7
Hawaiian Islands
Sierra Madre
Rio Grande

Canary Islands

Tropic of Cancer
Gulf of Mexico
Bahamas
A T L A N T I C

20°N
Hawaii
Yucatan
Cuba
Greater Antilles
Hispaniola
8605 Milwaukee Deep

Cape Verde Islands

Caribbean Sea

O C E A N

6
P A C I F I C
Panama Canal
Orinoco
Guiana Highlands

Fouta Djallo

0° Equator
Line Is
Galapagos Islands
Amazon
Chimborazo 6310

O C E A N
SOUTH

5
Marquesas Islands
Madeira
AMERICA
Tocantins

Polynesia
Society Is
Tuamotu Archipelago
Brazilian

Brazil Basin

20°S
Tropic of Capricorn
Andes
Gran Chaco
Paraguay
Parana
Highlands

He

Tonga Trench
Pitcairn Island
Easter Island
Peru-Chile Trench
Nevado Ojos del Salado 6908

4
Kermadec Trench
Southwest Pacific Basin
Cerro Aconcagua 6959
Pampas

Tris da

40°S
Rio de la Plata
Argentine Basin

Patagonia

3
Falkland Islands
South Georgia

60°S
Isla Grande Tierra del Fuego
C. Horn
Drake Passage

Antarctic Circle
Southeast Pacific Basin
Antarctic Peninsula
G Weddell Sea
H

A 2 B C D E G

80°S
160°W 140°W 120°W 100°W 80°W 60°W 40°W 20°W

Structure of the Earth

- Crust 6-50 km
- Upper Mantle (soft) 370 km
- Transitional Zone 600 km
- Lower Mantle (solid) 1700 km
- Outer Core (liquid) 2100 km
- Inner Core (solid) 1350 km

The earth is made up of three main layers.

The outer layer, known as the crust, ranges in thickness from a few kilometres under the oceans to almost 50 km under mountain ranges.

The middle layer, known as the mantle, makes up 82% of the earth's volume. At the centre (core) of the earth, temperatures reach 4300 °C.

North hemisph

PACIFIC OCEAN
Tropic of Cancer
NORTH AMERICA
North Pole
ASIA
Arctic Circle
SOUTH AMERICA
ATLANTIC OCEAN
EUROPE
INDIAN OCEAN
AFRICA

Key

Ice cap
8848 ▲ Mountain height (in metres)
10920 ▽ Ocean depth (in metres)

20°E 40°E 60°E 80°E 100°E 120°E 140°E 160°E 80°N

ARCTIC OCEAN

pitsbergen North Cape Barents Sea
gian
Scandinavia Yenisey Lena Arctic Circle 9
North Cape Balti
Lake Ladoga Ob' West Siberia
EUROPE Siberian Angara 60°N
Carpathian Mts Dnieper Ural Mts Plain Irtysh Altai Mts Selenga Kamchatka Sea of Kuril Trench 8
lps Volga Aral Lake A S I A Lake Pen. Okhotsk Vityaz Depth
Apennines Danube Black Sea Caucasus Sea Balkhash Baikal Gobi 10542
diterranean Sea Caspian Syr Darya Tien Shan Amur Sea of 40°N
Taurus Mts Sea Amu Darya Huang He Japan
Zagros Mts Hindu Kush K2 Kunlun Shan (East Sea) Honshū Ramapo Deep
Suez Euphrates 8611 Plateau Yellow Izu-Ogasawara Trench 9695
Nile The Gulf Indus Himalaya of Tibet Chang Jiang Sea PACIFIC 7
Tigris Annapurna 8091 ▲ ▲8848 East Tropic of Cancer
ra Arabian Dhaulagiri 8167 ▲ Kangchenjunga China
Tibesti Peninsula Thar Mt Everest 8586 Ganges Sea 20°N
Red Sea Desert Taiwan
AFRICA Blue Nile Deccan Bay South Philippines Challenger OCEAN 6
Adamawa Ethiopian Arabian of Western Ghats China Deep Caroline Is Marshall Is
Highlands Highlands Sea Bengal Sea 10057 10920 ▽
Benue White Nile Laccadive Mekong Philippine Cape
Congo Lake Is Peninsular Trench Johnson Mariana Trench Equator
Basin Turkana Sri Lanka Malaysia Depth
Congo Lake Mt Kenya ▲ Maldives Celebes Puncak Jaya 5
Victoria 5199 INDIAN Borneo Sea 5030 New Guinea Solomon Is
Lake Kilimanjaro ▲ Sumatra Celebes Banda OCEANIA
Tanganyika 5892 Seychelles OCEAN Java Sea New Guinea Gt Barrier Reef Fiji
Great Rift Valley Comoro Java 7125 Coral Sea
Bie Lake Islands Madagascar West Trench New 20°S
Plateau Nyasa Australian Great Caledonia
Zambezi Mauritius Basin Sandy Desert Tropic of Capricorn
Kalahari Réunion Australia Great Dividing Range
Orange Desert Great North 4
Drakensberg Victoria Desert Darling Island
Great Murray New
Cape of Australian Zealand 40°S
Good Hope Bight Tasman Aoraki
Prince Îles Îles Tasmania Sea (Mount Cook)
Edward Crozet Kerguelen South 3754
Is Island 3

SOUTHERN OCEAN
Antarctic Circle
K L M N O P Q R 2
TARCTICA
20°E 40°E 60°E 80°E 100°E 120°E 140°E 160°E 80°E

Scale 1 : 80 000 000
0 800 1600 2400 3200 km

Eckert IV projection

thern
nisphere

ATLANTIC AFRICA
OCEAN
SOUTH AMERICA INDIAN OCEAN
SOUTHERN OCEAN
South Pole
Tropic of Capricorn
Antarctic Circle
OCEANIA ASIA
PACIFIC OCEAN

World continents by area

North America
25 000 000 sq km

Europe
10 000 000 sq km

Asia
45 000 000 sq km

Africa
30 000 000 sq km

South America
18 000 000 sq km

Oceania
9 000 000 sq km

represents 1 million
square kilometres

Antarctica
12 000 000 sq km

? **What do you know about other places?**

GREENLAND (Denmark)

Nuuk (Godthåb)   Reykjavik   ICELAND

Arctic Circle

RUSSIAN FED.   U.S.A.

60°N   Anchorage

80°N   160°W   140°W   120°W   100°W   80°W   60°W   40°W   20°W

CANADA

Edmonton

Vancouver   Winnipeg

Seattle   Ottawa   Montreal

Toronto   Boston

Chicago   Detroit   New York

40°N   San Francisco   Pittsburgh   Philadelphia

Washington

UNITED STATES OF AMERICA

Los Angeles   Phoenix

KIM
Dubli
IRELAND

PORTUGAL   Lisbon   Rabat   MOR

Azores (Port.)

Dallas

Tropic of Cancer   Houston

Laäyoune

WESTERN SAHARA

20°N   Monterrey   Miami   THE BAHAMAS   Nassau

Guadalajara   MEXICO   Havana   CUBA

MAURITANIA

Hawaiian Islands (USA)   Mexico City   Belmopan   BELIZE   Kingston   DOMINICAN REP.   San Juan

GUATEMALA   HAITI   PUERTO RICO (USA)

Guatemala City   HONDURAS   JAMAICA

Nouakchott

CAPE VERDE   SENEGAL   Dakar   Bamo

EL SALVADOR   Tegucigalpa   NICARAGUA

THE GAMBIA   Bissau   Ouaga

6   Managua   Caracas   TRINIDAD & TOBAGO   GUINEA-BISSAU   GUINEA

COSTA RICA   Panama City   Port of Spain   Conakry   Freetown   Yamo

San José   VENEZUELA   SIERRA LEONE

PANAMA   Georgetown   GUY.   Paramaribo   Monrovia

Bogotá   SUR.   Cayenne   LIBERIA

PACIFIC   COLOMBIA   FR.G.

Quito

OCEAN   ECUADOR   ATLANT

Equator   Galapagos Is (Ec)

KIRIBATI   BRAZIL   Recife

Marquesas Is (Fr)   PERU   OCEAN

5   SAMOA   French Polynesia   Lima

Cook Islands (NZ)   Society Is (Fr)   La Paz   Brasilia

Tahiti   Tuamoto Is   BOLIVIA   Belo Horizonte

TONGA   Sucre   Río de Janeiro

20°S   Tropic of Capricorn   PARAGUAY   São Paulo

Pitcairn Island (UK)   Asunción

4   Easter I. (Chile)

Santiago   ARGENTINA   URUGUAY

Buenos Aires   Montevideo

Falkland Islands (UK)

South Georgia (UK)

Abbreviations of Country Names

SOUTH AMERICA	EUROPE	MA. MACEDONIA
FR.G. FRENCH GUIANA	A. ANDORRA	MO. MOLDOVA
GUY. GUYANA	ALB. ALBANIA	NETH. NETHERLANDS
SUR. SURINAME	AUS. AUSTRIA	R.F. RUSSIAN FEDERATION
	BEL. BELGIUM	S. SLOVENIA
AFRICA	BELA. BELARUS	SER. SERBIA
B. BURUNDI	B.H. BOSNIA-HERZEGOVINA	SL. SLOVAKIA
BE. BENIN	CR. CROATIA	SW. SWITZERLAND
BUR. BURKINA FASO	CZ. CZECH REPUBLIC	
CAM. CAMEROON	DEN. DENMARK	ASIA
C.D'I. CÔTE D'IVOIRE	EST. ESTONIA	AR. ARMENIA
EQ. G. EQUATORIAL GUINEA	GER. GERMANY	AZ. AZERBAIJAN
	H. HUNGARY	CYP. CYPRUS
GH. GHANA	K. KOSOVO	GEO. GEORGIA
R. RWANDA	LAT. LATVIA	IS. ISRAEL
T. TOGO	LITH. LITHUANIA	JOR. JORDAN
	LUX. LUXEMBOURG	LEB. LEBANON
	M. MONTENEGRO	U.A.E. UNITED ARAB EMIRATES

Time Comparisons

Time varies around the world due to the earth's rotation causing different parts of the world to be in light or darkness at an one time. To account for this, the world is divided into twenty-four Standard Time Zones based on 15° intervals of longitude

1:00am	2:00am	3:00am	4:00am	5:00am	6:00am	7:00am	8:00am	9:00am	10:00am	11:00am	no
Samoa Tonga (next day)	Hawaiian Is Cook Is Tahiti	Anchorage	Vancouver Seattle Los Angeles	Edmonton Phoenix	Winnipeg Chicago Mexico City	New York Miami Lima	Puerto Rico La Paz Asunción	Nuuk Brasília Buenos Aires	South Georgia	Azores Cape Verde	Reyk Lon Free

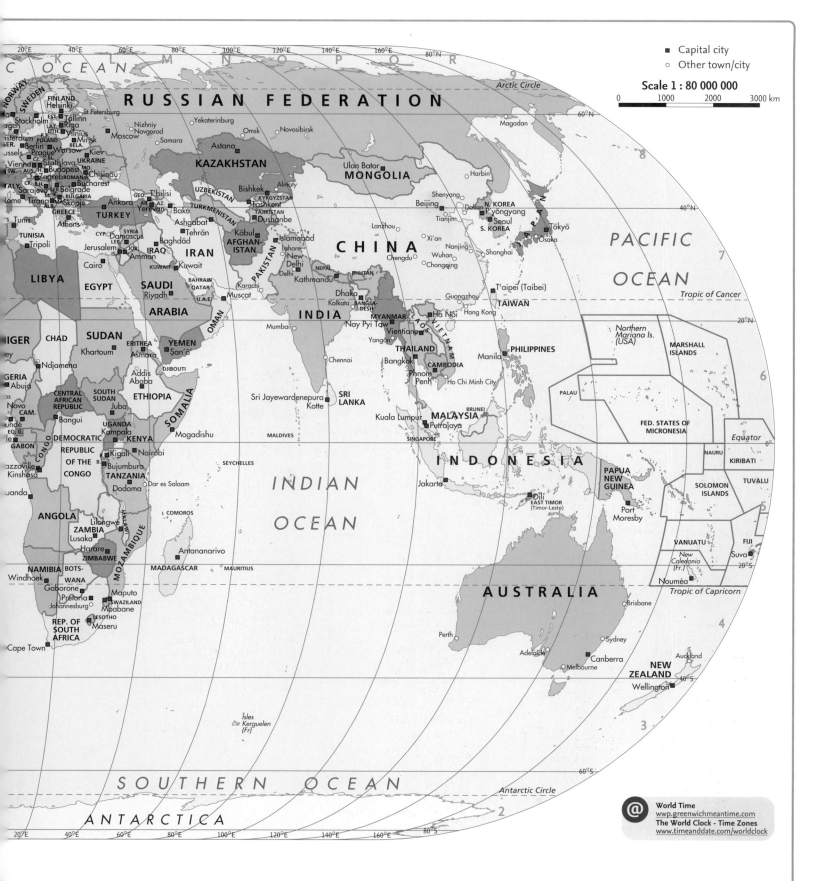

■ Capital city
○ Other town/city

Scale 1 : 80 000 000

0   1000   2000   3000 km

@ **World Time**
wwp.greenwichmeantime.com
The World Clock - Time Zones
www.timeanddate.com/worldclock

e table below gives examples of times observed at different parts of the world when it is 12 noon in the zone at the Greenwich Meridian (0° longitude).
e time at 0° is known as Greenwich Mean Time (GMT).

...m	2:00pm	3:00pm	4:00pm	5:00pm	6:00pm	7:00pm	8:00pm	9:00pm	10:00pm	11:00pm	midnight
...lo ...ris ...nasa	Helsinki Cairo Cape Town	Addis Ababa Riyadh Dodoma	Moscow U.A.E. Mauritius	Tashkent Dushanbe Karachi	Yekaterinburg Almaty Dhaka	Novosibirsk Bangkok Jakarta	Ulan Bator Hong Kong Perth	P'yŏngyang Tōkyō Palau	Port Moresby Brisbane Canberra	Solomon Is Vanuatu New Caledonia	Marshall Is Fiji Wellington

Eckert IV projection

Key

Earthquakes and volcanoes

- ● Earthquake
- ▲ Volcano
- —— Plate boundary
- ← → Direction of movement

Storms and floods

- ← Typical storm path
- ∿ Rivers that experience major flooding
- ▭ Country affected annually by severe flooding
- ◊ Severe floods causing over 1000 deaths in 1 year (1985–2011)
- ◊ Severe floods causing 500–1000 deaths in 1 year (1985–2011)

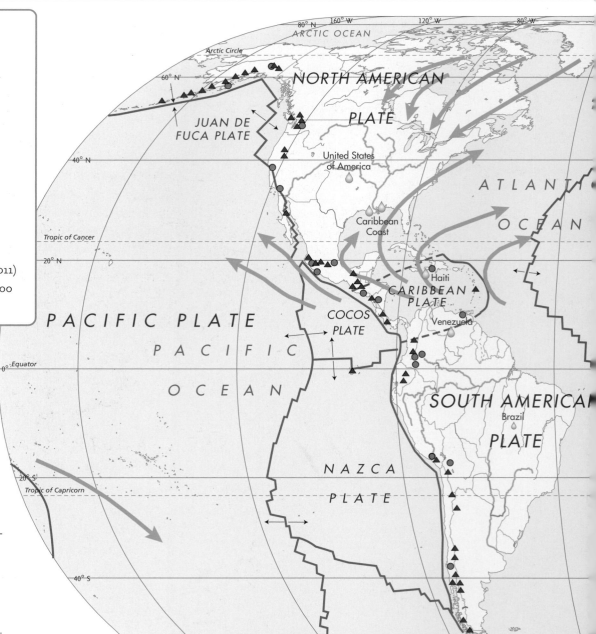

Plates

The earth's crust is broken into huge plates which fit together like parts of a giant jigsaw. These float on the semi-molten rock below. The boundaries of the plates are marked by lines of volcanoes and earthquake activity.

Diverging Plates

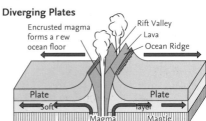

Diverging convection currents

Converging Plates

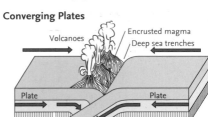

Converging convection currents

Shearing Plates

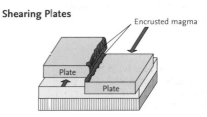

Currents moving past each other

Plate Structure: Asia to South America

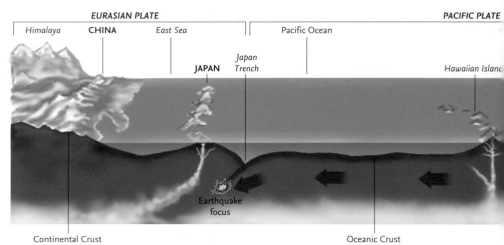

? **What causes natural disasters?**

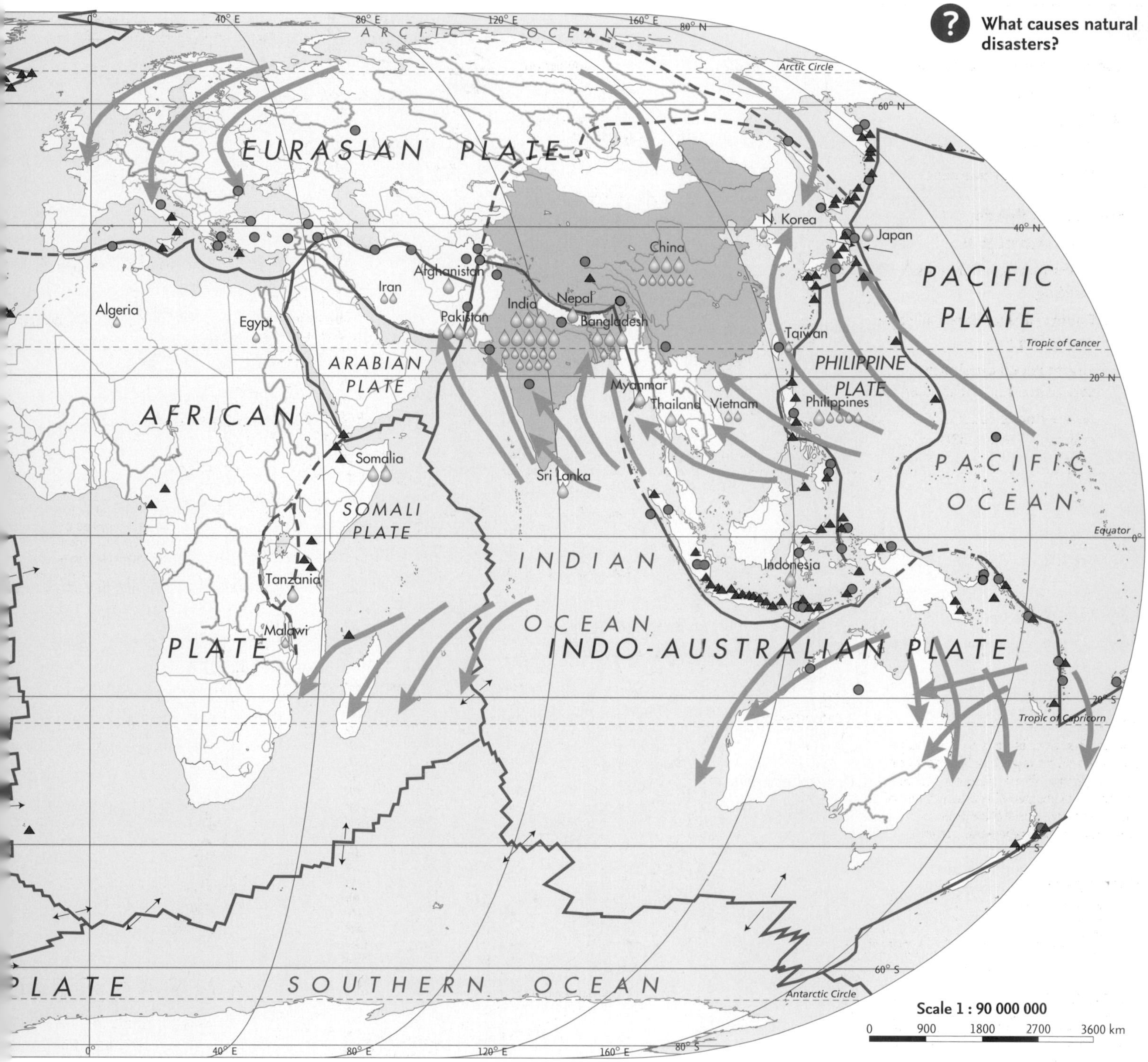

ARCTIC OCEAN

Arctic Circle

EURASIAN PLATE

60° N

N. Korea

Japan

40° N

China

PACIFIC PLATE

Afghanistan

Iran

India   Nepal

Pakistan   Bangladesh

Taiwan

Tropic of Cancer

Algeria

Egypt

ARABIAN PLATE

Myanmar

Thailand   Vietnam

PHILIPPINE PLATE

Philippines

20° N

AFRICAN

Somalia

SOMALI PLATE

Sri Lanka

PACIFIC OCEAN

Equator

Tanzania

INDIAN

Indonesia

Malawi

PLATE

OCEAN

INDO-AUSTRALIAN PLATE

Tropic of Capricorn

20° S

SOUTHERN OCEAN

60° S

Antarctic Circle

Scale 1 : 90 000 000

0   900   1800   2700   3600 km

@ **USGS Volcano Hazards Program**
volcanoes.usgs.gov
USGS National Earthquake Information Center
earthquake.usgs.gov/regional/neic
British Geological Survey
www.bgs.ac.uk

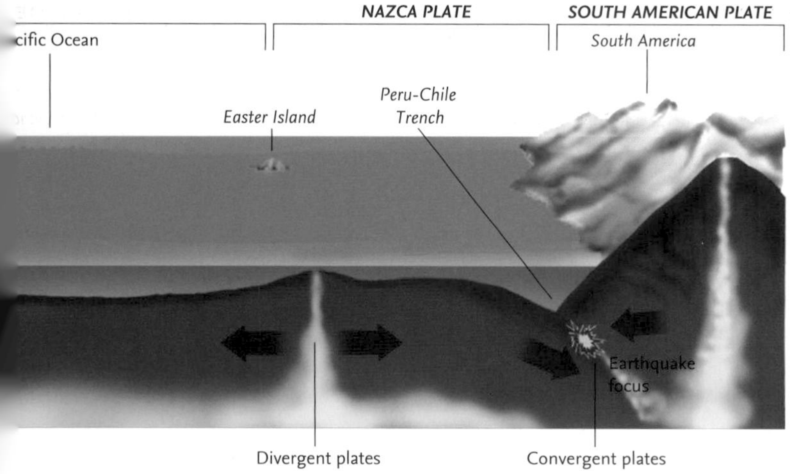

NAZCA PLATE   SOUTH AMERICAN PLATE

Pacific Ocean   South America

Easter Island   Peru-Chile Trench

Earthquakes

Earthquakes occur most frequently along the junction of plates which make up the earth's crust.
They are caused by the release of stress which builds up at the plate edges. When shock waves from these movements reach the surface they are felt as earthquakes which may result in severe damage to property or loss of lives.

Volcanoes

The greatest number of volcanoes are located in the Pacific 'Ring of Fire'. Violent eruptions often occur when two plates collide and the heat generated forces molten rock (magma) upwards through weaknesses in the earth's crust.

Earthquake focus

Divergent plates   Convergent plates

Eckert IV projection

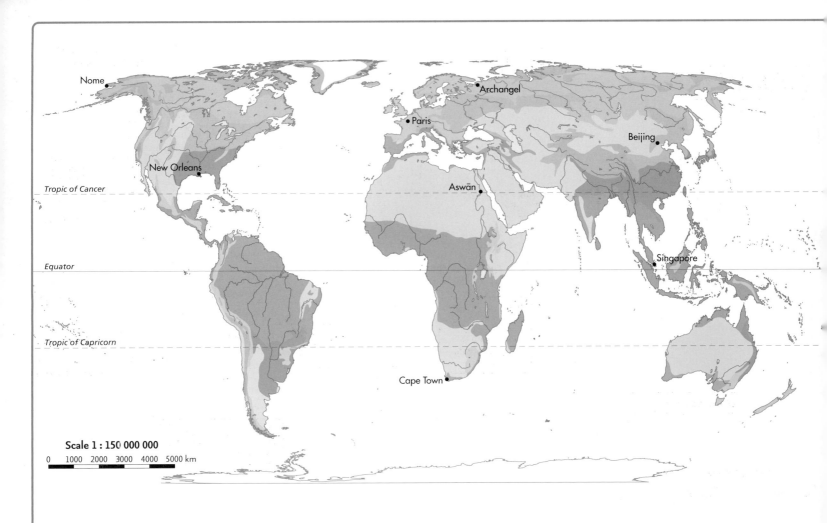

Climate types

- **Ice cap** (very cold and dry)
- **Tundra and mountain** (very cold winters, altitude affects climate)
- **Subarctic** (rainy climate, with long cold winters)
- **Continental** (rainy climate, cold winters, mild / warm summers)
- **Temperate** (rainy climate, mild winters, warm summers)
- **Mediterranean** (rainy mild winters, dry hot summers)
- **Subtropical** (wet warm winters, hot summers)
- **Tropical** (constantly hot and wet)
- **Dry / Arid and Desert** (dry all year)
- • Climate station

@ World Meteorological Organization
www.wmo.ch
Met Office World Weather
www.metoffice.gov.uk/weather/world/

Climate graphs

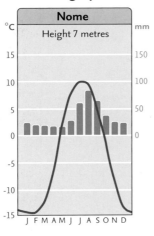
Nome — Height 7 metres

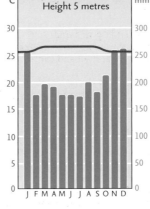
Singapore — Height 5 metres

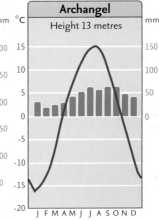
Archangel — Height 13 metres

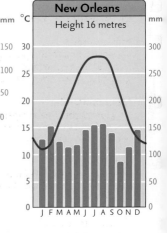
New Orleans — Height 16 metres

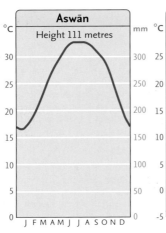
Aswān — Height 111 metres

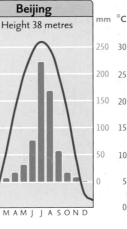
Beijing — Height 38 metres

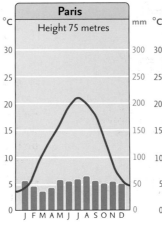
Paris — Height 75 metres

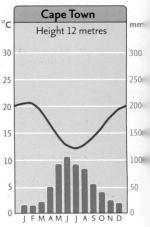
Cape Town — Height 12 metres

Scale 1 : 150 000 000
0 1000 2000 3000 4000 5000 km

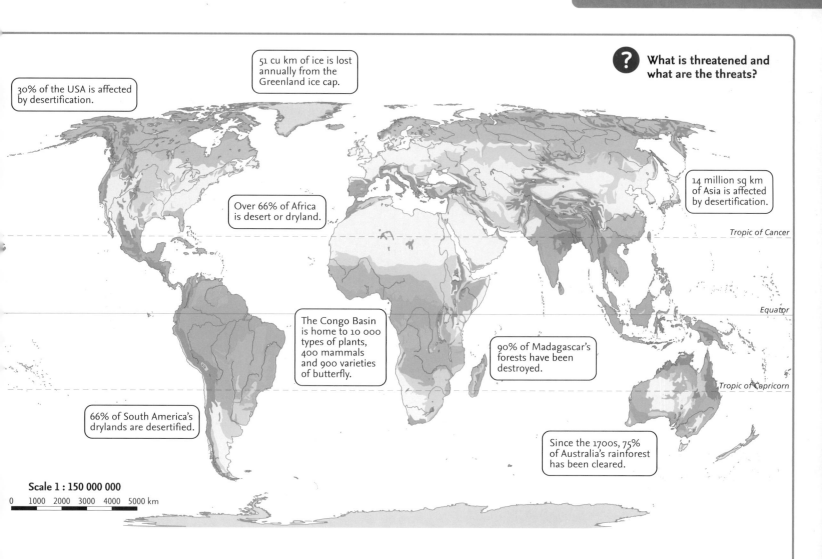

30% of the USA is affected by desertification.

51 cu km of ice is lost annually from the Greenland ice cap.

? What is threatened and what are the threats?

Over 66% of Africa is desert or dryland.

14 million sq km of Asia is affected by desertification.

Tropic of Cancer

The Congo Basin is home to 10 000 types of plants, 400 mammals and 900 varieties of butterfly.

90% of Madagascar's forests have been destroyed.

Equator

66% of South America's drylands are desertified.

Tropic of Capricorn

Since the 1700s, 75% of Australia's rainforest has been cleared.

Scale 1 : 150 000 000

0 1000 2000 3000 4000 5000 km

Types of vegetation

Ice cap and ice shelf
Extremely cold. No vegetation.

Arctic tundra
Very cold climate. Simple vegetation such as mosses, lichens, grasses and flowering herbs.

Mountain/Alpine
Very low night-time temperatures. Only a few dwarf trees and small leafed shrubs can grow.

Mediterranean
Mild winters and dry summers. Vegetation is mixed shrubs and herbaceous plants.

Savanna grassland
Warm or hot climate. Tropical grasslands with scattered thorn bushes or trees.

Temperate grassland
Grassland is the main vegetation. Summers are hot and winters cold.

Desert
Hot with little rainfall. Very sparse vegetation except cacti and grasses adapted to the harsh conditions.

Boreal/Taiga forest
Found between 50° and 70°N. Low temperatures. Vegetation consists of cold tolerant evergreen conifers.

Coniferous forest
Dense forests of pine, spruce and larch.

Temperate grassland
Grassland is the main vegetation. Summers are hot and winters cold.

Tropical forest
Dense rainforest found in areas of high rainfall near the equator.

Dry tropical forest
Semi deciduous trees with low shrubs and bushes.

Sub tropical forest
Rainfall is seasonal. Vegetation is mainly hard leaf evergreen forest.

Monsoon forest
Areas which experience Monsoon rain. All trees are deciduous.

Rainforests which once grew on 14% of the land surface now cover 6%. Rainforests could disappear completely within 100 years if the current rate of deforestation continues.
Animal habitats are shrinking due to pollution, logging, harmful development and global warming.

World ecosystems

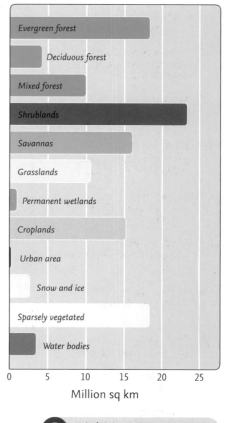

Million sq km

@ **United Nations Environment Programme**
www.unep.org
World Conservation Monitoring Centre
www.unep-wcmc.org
World Resources Institute Earthtrends
earthtrends.wri.org

Global warming

The average temperature of the earth is rising, a process called global warming. Global warming is believed to cause changes to the world's climate which could have serious effects on the environment and people's lives.

Key

Farmland		**Signs of global warming**	
Wetter than before		Spreading diseases	
Drier than before		Earlier spring	
Evidence of global warming		Plant and animal habitat shifts	
Heat waves		Coral damage	
Ocean warming		Heavy rainfall, snowfall and flooding	
Glaciers melting		Drought and fires	
Polar temperature rise			

Global temperature difference 1950-2080

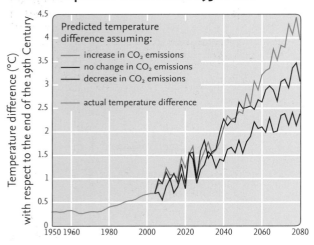

Temperature difference (°C) with respect to the end of the 19th Century

Predicted temperature difference assuming:
— increase in CO_2 emissions
— no change in CO_2 emissions
— decrease in CO_2 emissions
— actual temperature difference

4.5 4 3.5 3 2.5 2 1.5 1 0.5 0
1950 1960   1980   2000   2020   2040   2060   2080

Better farming conditions

Shrinking glaciers

Change in ocean currents

Tropic of Cancer

More powerful hurricanes

Equator

Worse farming conditions

Tropic of Capricorn

The Greenhouse Effect

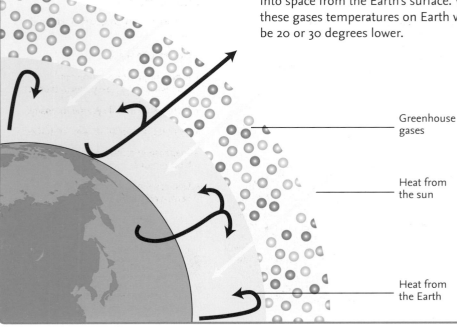

Greenhouse gases build up in the Earth's atmosphere, stopping heat bouncing back into space from the Earth's surface. Without these gases temperatures on Earth would be 20 or 30 degrees lower.

Greenhouse gases

Heat from the sun

Heat from the Earth

Fossil fuels are the primary source of carbon dioxide emissions which, along with the other greenhouse gases, are believed to be the principal cause of global climate change.

Evidence of climate change

- Warming oceans
- Shrinking ice sheets
- Declining Arctic sea ice
- Global surface temperature rise
- Sea level rise
- Retreating glaciers
- Ocean acidification
- Extreme events

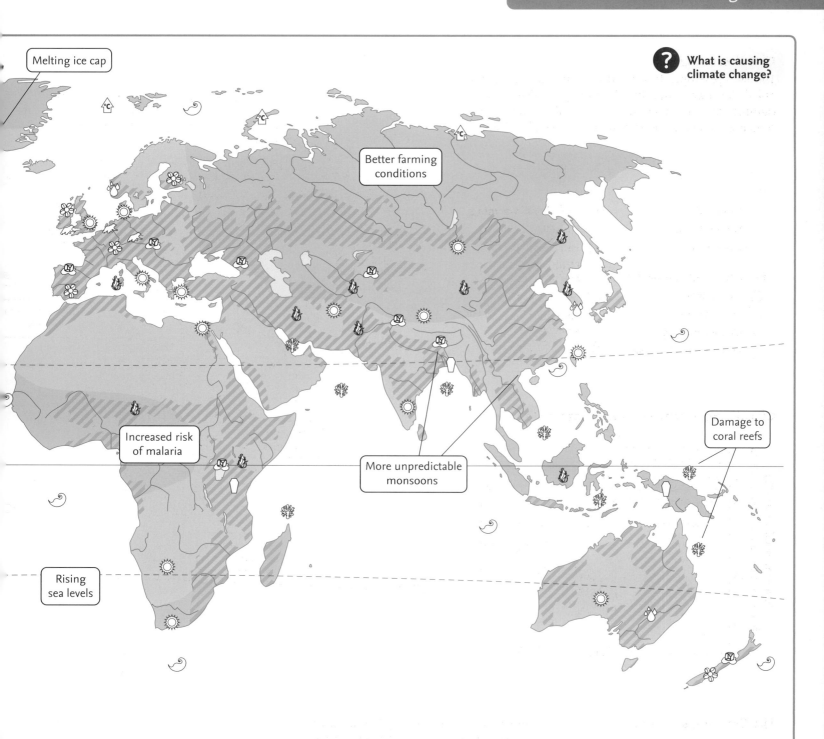

Melting ice cap

? What is causing climate change?

Better farming conditions

Increased risk of malaria

More unpredictable monsoons

Damage to coral reefs

Rising sea levels

Projected temperature change

These maps show projected change in annual mean surface air temperature given moderate growth in CO2 emissions, for three time periods, compared with the average temperature for 1980-1999.

0 1 2 3 4 5 6 7 8°C

2011-2030

2046-2065

2080-2099

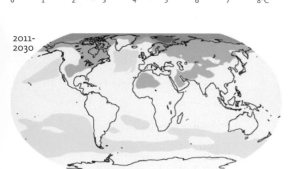

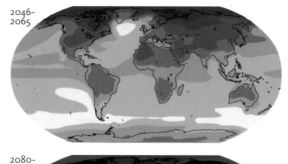

Future trends

- Reduced snow cover and increased thaw.

- Decrease in sea ice.

- More frequent hot extremes, heat waves and heavy precipitation.

- Increased tropical cyclone intensity.

- Increase in rainfall in high altitudes.

- Decrease in rainfall in sub tropical land regions.

- Decrease in water resources in semi-arid areas.

@ World Meteorological Organization
www.wmo.int
Met Office World Weather
www.metoffice.gov.uk/weather/world/
Intergovernmental Panel on Climate Change
www.ipcc.ch

Key

Desertification
Existing deserts
Areas at risk of desertification

Deforestation
Existing tropical forests
Forests destroyed since 1940

Bushfires
Recent major forest fires

Water pollution
Coastal pollution
River pollution
Major city with air pollution

Deforestation

Impacts of deforestation

- Flood water carries away unprotected soil

- Without vegetation to soak up water, heavy rain causes floods

- Without humus from rotting leaves, the soil becomes poorer

- Rivers silt up, causing floods and clogging dams

- Burning trees release CO_2 into the atmosphere, adding to 'greenhouse' gases

- Fierce sunshine dries out the earth, making it useless for crops

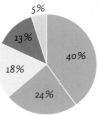

Causes of tropical deforestation 2000-2005

5%
13%
18%
24%
40%

- Small-holder agriculture
- Cattle pasture
- Large-scale agriculture
- Logging
- Other

Change in forest area

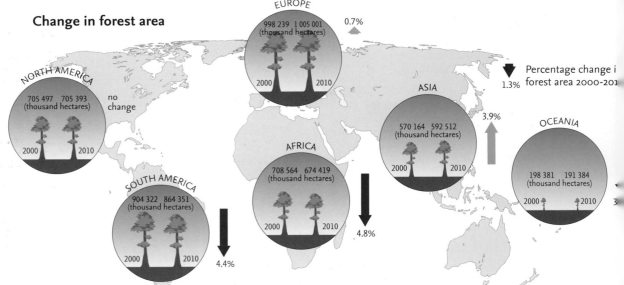

EUROPE
998 239 1 005 001
(thousand hectares)
2000   2010
0.7%

NORTH AMERICA
705 497   705 393
(thousand hectares)
2000   2010
no change

ASIA
570 164   592 512
(thousand hectares)
2000   2010
3.9%

AFRICA
708 564   674 419
(thousand hectares)
2000   2010
4.8%

OCEANIA
198 381   191 384
(thousand hectares)
2000   2010

SOUTH AMERICA
904 322   864 351
(thousand hectares)
2000   2010
4.4%

Percentage change i
forest area 2000-201
1.3%

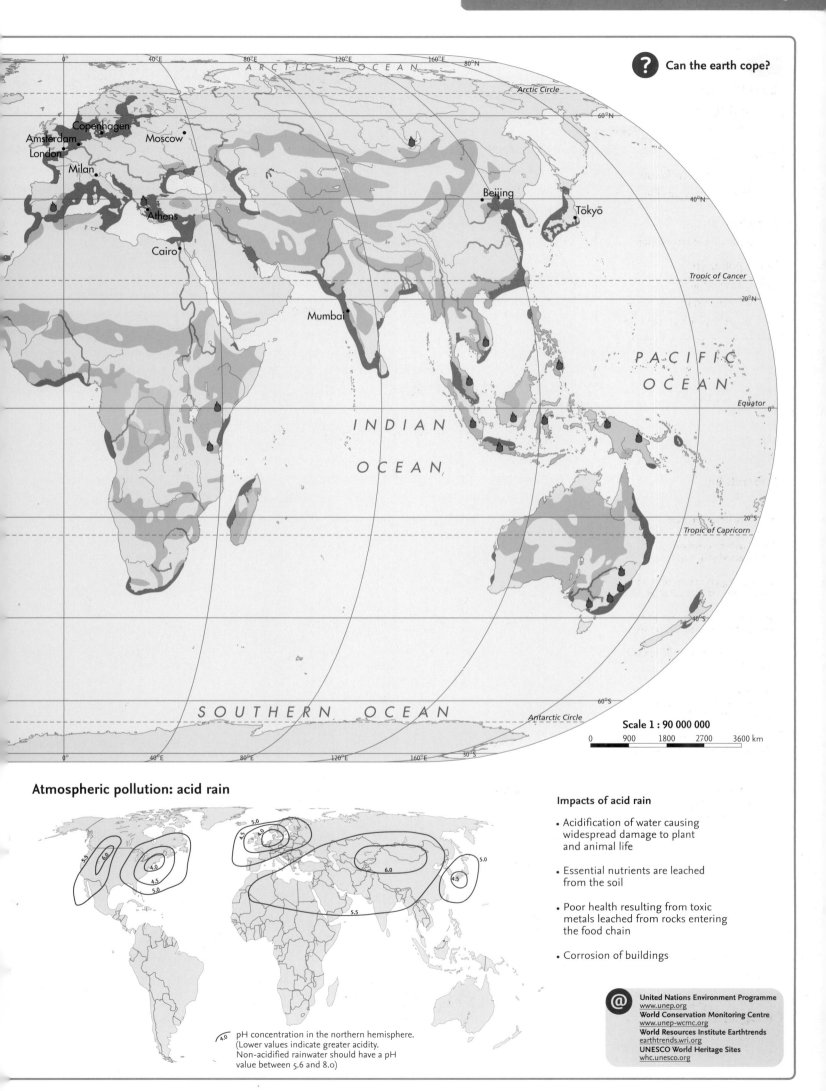

? Can the earth cope?

Atmospheric pollution: acid rain

Impacts of acid rain

- Acidification of water causing widespread damage to plant and animal life

- Essential nutrients are leached from the soil

- Poor health resulting from toxic metals leached from rocks entering the food chain

- Corrosion of buildings

4.0 pH concentration in the northern hemisphere. (Lower values indicate greater acidity. Non-acidified rainwater should have a pH value between 5.6 and 8.0)

@ **United Nations Environment Programme** www.unep.org
World Conservation Monitoring Centre www.unep-wcmc.org
World Resources Institute Earthtrends earthtrends.wri.org
UNESCO World Heritage Sites whc.unesco.org

Scale 1 : 90 000 000

0 900 1800 2700 3600 km

Eckert IV projection

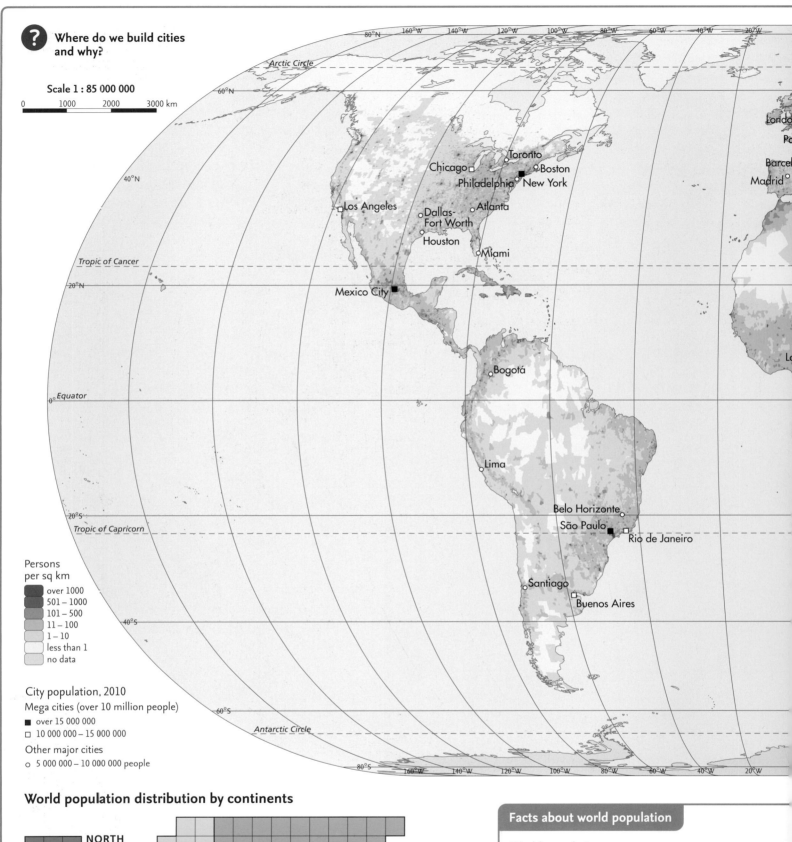

? Where do we build cities and why?

Scale 1 : 85 000 000

0   1000   2000   3000 km

Persons
per sq km

- over 1000
- 501 – 1000
- 101 – 500
- 11 – 100
- 1 – 10
- less than 1
- no data

City population, 2010
Mega cities (over 10 million people)
- ■ over 15 000 000
- □ 10 000 000 – 15 000 000

Other major cities
- o 5 000 000 – 10 000 000 people

World population distribution by continents

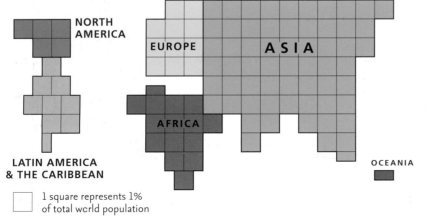

NORTH AMERICA

EUROPE

ASIA

AFRICA

OCEANIA

LATIN AMERICA & THE CARIBBEAN

□ 1 square represents 1% of total world population

Facts about world population

World population, 2011	6 974 036
World population, 2050	9 306 127
Population 60 years and over, 2011	12
Population 60 years and over, 2050	26
Population under 15 years, 2011	26
Population under 15 years, 2050	20
Life expectancy, 2010-2015	
Male life expectancy, 2010-2015	
Female life expectancy, 2010-2015	

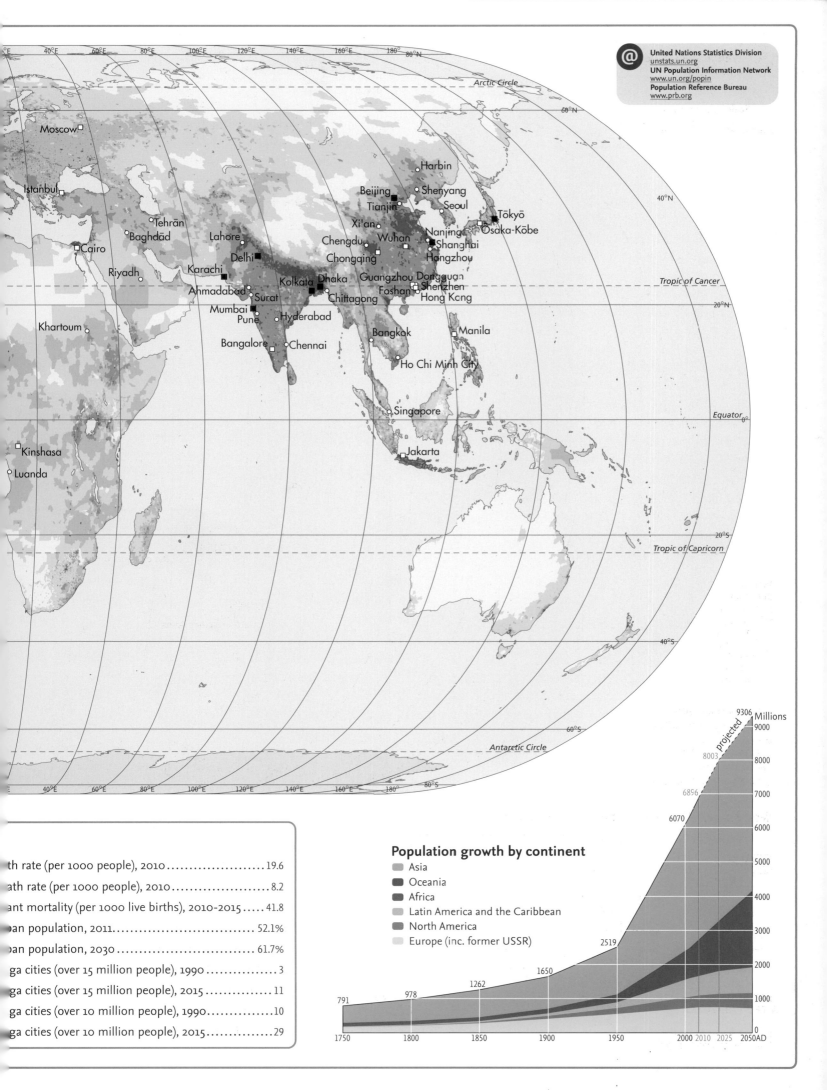

United Nations Statistics Division
unstats.un.org
UN Population Information Network
www.un.org/popin
Population Reference Bureau
www.prb.org

Moscow

Istanbul

Tehrān

Baghdād

Cairo

Riyadh

Lahore

Delhi

Karachi

Khartoum

Ahmadabad

Mumbai

Pune

Surat

Hyderabad

Bangalore

Chennai

Kolkata

Dhaka

Chittagong

Kinshasa

Luanda

Harbin

Beijing

Tianjin

Shenyang

Seoul

Xi'an

Wuhan

Chengdu

Chongqing

Nanjing

Shanghai

Hangzhou

Tōkyō

Osaka-Kōbe

Guangzhou

Dongguan

Foshan

Shenzhen

Hong Kong

Bangkok

Manila

Ho Chi Minh City

Singapore

Jakarta

Arctic Circle

Tropic of Cancer

Equator

Tropic of Capricorn

Antarctic Circle

th rate (per 1000 people), 2010 .... 19.6

ath rate (per 1000 people), 2010 .... 8.2

ant mortality (per 1000 live births), 2010-2015 ..... 41.8

an population, 2011 .... 52.1%

an population, 2030 .... 61.7%

ga cities (over 15 million people), 1990 3

ga cities (over 15 million people), 2015 11

ga cities (over 10 million people), 1990 10

ga cities (over 10 million people), 2015 29

Population growth by continent

- Asia
- Oceania
- Africa
- Latin America and the Caribbean
- North America
- Europe (inc. former USSR)

projected

9306 Millions

9000

8003

8000

6896

7000

6070

6000

5000

4000

2519

3000

1650

2000

1262

978

791

1000

0

1750   1800   1850   1900   1950   2000 2010 2025   2050AD

Eckert IV projection

Flag	Country	Capital city	Area sq km	Total population 2011	Density persons per sq km 2011	Birth rate per 1000 population 2010	Life expectancy in years 2010	Urban population % 2011	Population change annual % 2011
	Afghanistan	Kābul	652 225	32 358 000	50	44	48	24	2.7
	Albania	Tirana	28 748	3 216 000	112	13	77	53	0.4
	Algeria	Algiers	2 381 741	35 980 000	15	20	73	73	1.4
	Angola	Luanda	1 246 700	19 618 000	16	42	51	59	2.8
	Antigua & Barbuda	St John's	442	90 000	204	..	..	30	1.0
	Argentina	Buenos Aires	2 766 889	40 765 000	15	17	76	92	0.9
	Armenia	Yerevan	29 800	3 100 000	104	15	74	64	0.3
	Australia	Canberra	7 692 024	22 606 000	3	13	82	89	1.4
	Austria	Vienna	83 855	8 413 000	100	9	80	68	0.3
	Azerbaijan	Baku	86 600	9 306 000	107	19	71	54	1.2
	Bahamas, The	Nassau	13 939	347 000	25	15	75	84	1.2
	Bahrain	Manama	691	1 324 000	1916	20	75	89	4.8
	Bangladesh	Dhaka	143 998	150 494 000	1045	20	69	28	1.2
	Barbados	Bridgetown	430	274 000	637	11	77	44	0.2
	Belarus	Minsk	207 600	9 559 000	46	11	70	75	-0.2
	Belgium	Brussels	30 520	10 754 000	352	12	80	97	1.0
	Belize	Belmopan	22 965	318 000	14	25	76	45	3.4
	Benin	Porto-Novo	112 620	9 100 000	81	40	56	45	2.8
	Bhutan	Thimphu	46 620	738 000	16	20	67	36	1.7
	Bolivia	La Paz/Sucre	1 098 581	10 088 000	9	26	66	67	1.6
	Bosnia-Herzegovina	Sarajevo	51 130	3 752 000	73	9	75	48	-0.2
	Botswana	Gaborone	581 370	2 031 000	3	24	53	62	1.2
	Brazil	Brasília	8 514 879	196 655 000	23	15	73	85	0.9
	Brunei	Bandar Seri Begawan	5 765	406 000	70	19	78	76	1.7
	Bulgaria	Sofia	110 994	7 446 000	67	10	74	73	-0.8
	Burkina Faso	Ouagadougou	274 200	16 968 000	62	43	55	27	3.0
	Burundi	Bujumbura	27 835	8 575 000	308	34	50	11	2.3
	Cambodia	Phnom Penh	181 035	14 305 000	79	22	63	20	1.2
	Cameroon	Yaoundé	475 442	20 030 000	42	36	51	52	2.2
	Canada	Ottawa	9 984 670	34 350 000	3	11	81	81	1.0
	Cape Verde	Praia	4 033	501 000	124	21	74	63	0.9
	Central African Republic	Bangui	622 436	4 487 000	7	35	48	39	1.9
	Chad	Ndjamena	1 284 000	11 525 000	9	45	49	22	2.6
	Chile	Santiago	756 945	17 270 000	23	14	79	89	0.9
	China	Beijing	9 584 492	1 332 079 000	139	12	73	51	0.5
	Colombia	Bogotá	1 141 748	46 927 000	41	20	73	75	1.4
	Comoros	Moroni	1 862	754 000	405	38	61	28	2.6
	Congo	Brazzaville	342 000	4 140 000	12	35	57	64	2.4
	Congo, Dem. Rep. of the	Kinshasa	2 345 410	67 758 000	29	43	48	34	2.7
	Costa Rica	San José	51 100	4 727 000	93	16	79	65	1.4
	Côte d'Ivoire	Yamoussoukro	322 463	20 153 000	62	34	55	51	2.1
	Croatia	Zagreb	56 538	4 396 000	78	10	76	58	-0.2
	Cuba	Havana	110 860	11 254 000	102	10	79	75	0.0
	Cyprus	Nicosia	9 251	1 117 000	121	12	79	71	1.2
	Czech Republic	Prague	78 864	10 534 000	134	11	77	73	0.2
	Denmark	Copenhagen	43 075	5 573 000	129	11	79	87	0.5
	Djibouti	Djibouti	23 200	906 000	39	29	58	77	1.9

.. no data availa

Flag	Country	Capital city	Area sq km	Total population 2011	Density persons per sq km 2011	Birth rate per 1000 population 2010	Life expectancy in years 2010	Urban population % 2011	Population change annual % 2011
	Dominica	Roseau	750	68 000	91	..	..	67	-0.1
	Dominican Republic	Santo Domingo	48 442	10 056 000	208	22	73	70	1.3
	East Timor	Dili	14 874	1 154 000	78	38	62	28	2.9
	Ecuador	Quito	272 045	14 666 000	54	21	75	67	1.4
	Egypt	Cairo	1 001 450	82 537 000	82	23	73	44	1.7
	El Salvador	San Salvador	21 041	6 227 000	296	20	72	65	0.6
	Equatorial Guinea	Malabo	28 051	720 000	26	37	51	40	2.8
	Eritrea	Asmara	117 400	5 415 000	46	36	61	21	3.0
	Estonia	Tallinn	45 200	1 341 000	30	12	75	70	0.0
	Ethiopia	Addis Ababa	1 133 880	84 734 000	75	31	59	17	2.1
	Fiji	Suva	18 330	868 000	47	22	69	52	0.9
	Finland	Helsinki	338 145	5 385 000	16	11	80	84	0.4
	France	Paris	543 965	63 126 000	116	13	81	86	0.6
	Gabon	Libreville	267 667	1 534 000	6	27	62	86	1.9
	Gambia, The	Banjul	11 295	1 776 000	157	38	58	57	2.7
	Georgia	T'bilisi	69 700	4 329 000	62	12	73	53	0.7
	Germany	Berlin	357 022	82 163 000	230	8	80	74	-0.1
	Ghana	Accra	238 537	24 966 000	105	32	64	52	2.3
	Greece	Athens	131 957	11 390 000	86	10	80	61	-0.1
	Grenada	St George's	378	105 000	278	19	76	39	0.4
	Guatemala	Guatemala City	108 890	14 757 000	136	32	71	50	2.5
	Guinea	Conakry	245 857	10 222 000	42	39	54	35	2.4
	Guinea-Bissau	Bissau	36 125	1 547 000	43	38	48	44	2.1
	Guyana	Georgetown	214 969	756 000	4	18	70	28	0.2
	Haiti	Port-au-Prince	27 750	10 124 000	365	27	62	53	1.3
	Honduras	Tegucigalpa	112 088	7 755 000	69	27	73	52	2.0
	Hungary	Budapest	93 030	9 966 000	107	9	74	69	-0.3
	Iceland	Reykjavík	102 820	324 000	3	15	81	94	0.3
	India	New Delhi	3 064 898	1 241 492 000	405	22	65	31	1.4
	Indonesia	Jakarta	1 919 445	242 326 000	126	18	69	51	1.0
	Iran	Tehrān	1 648 000	74 799 000	45	17	73	69	1.1
	Iraq	Baghdād	438 317	32 665 000	75	35	68	67	2.9
	Ireland	Dublin	70 282	4 526 000	64	17	80	62	0.3
	Israel	*Jerusalem	20 770	7 562 000	364	22	82	92	1.8
	Italy	Rome	301 245	60 789 000	202	9	82	68	0.5
	Jamaica	Kingston	10 991	2 751 000	250	16	73	52	0.3
	Japan	Tōkyō	377 727	126 497 000	335	9	83	91	0.3
	Jordan	'Ammān	89 206	6 330 000	71	25	73	83	2.2
	Kazakhstan	Astana	2 717 300	16 207 000	6	22	68	54	1.4
	Kenya	Nairobi	582 646	41 610 000	71	38	56	24	2.7
	Kiribati	Bairiki	717	101 000	141	..	..	44	1.5
	Kosovo	Priština	10 908	2 180 686	200	19	70	..	1.0
	Kuwait	Kuwait	17 818	2 818 000	158	18	75	98	2.9
	Kyrgyzstan	Bishkek	198 500	5 393 000	27	27	69	35	1.1
	Laos	Vientiane	236 800	6 288 000	27	23	67	34	1.4
	Latvia	Rīga	64 589	2 243 000	35	9	73	68	-0.9
	Lebanon	Beirut	10 452	4 259 000	407	15	72	87	0.7

Flag	Country	Capital city	Area sq km	Total population 2011	Density persons per sq km 2011	Birth rate per 1000 population 2010	Life expectancy in years 2010	Urban population % 2011	Population change annual % 2011
	Lesotho	Maseru	30 355	2 194 000	72	28	47	28	1.0
	Liberia	Monrovia	111 369	4 129 000	37	39	56	48	3.3
	Libya	Tripoli	1 759 540	6 423 000	4	23	75	78	1.1
	Liechtenstein	Vaduz	160	36 000	225	9	..	14	0.8
	Lithuania	Vilnius	65 200	3 307 000	51	11	73	67	-2.6
	Luxembourg	Luxembourg	2 586	516 000	200	12	80	85	2.0
	Macedonia	Skopje	25 713	2 064 000	80	11	75	59	0.2
	Madagascar	Antananarivo	587 041	21 315 000	36	35	66	33	2.9
	Malawi	Lilongwe	118 484	15 381 000	130	44	53	16	3.2
	Malaysia	Kuala Lumpur/Putrajaya	332 965	28 859 000	87	20	74	73	1.6
	Maldives	Male	298	320 000	1074	17	77	41	1.3
	Mali	Bamako	1 240 140	15 840 000	13	46	51	35	3.0
	Malta	Valletta	316	418 000	1323	10	81	95	0.7
	Marshall Islands	Dalap-Uliga-Darrit	181	55 000	304	..	..	72	1.4
	Mauritania	Nouakchott	1 030 700	3 542 000	3	34	58	42	2.3
	Mauritius	Port Louis	2 040	1 307 000	641	12	73	42	0.4
	Mexico	Mexico City	1 972 545	114 793 000	58	20	77	78	1.2
	Micronesia, Fed. States of	Palikir	701	112 000	160	25	69	23	0.4
	Moldova	Chișinău	33 700	3 545 000	105	12	69	48	-0.1
	Mongolia	Ulan Bator	1 565 000	2 800 000	2	23	68	68	1.6
	Montenegro	Podgorica	13 812	632 000	46	12	74	63	0.1
	Morocco	Rabat	446 550	32 273 000	72	20	72	57	1.0
	Mozambique	Maputo	799 380	23 930 000	30	38	50	31	2.3
	Myanmar	Nay Pyi Taw	676 577	48 337 000	71	17	65	33	0.8
	Namibia	Windhoek	824 292	2 324 000	3	26	62	38	1.8
	Nepal	Kathmandu	147 181	30 486 000	207	24	68	17	1.7
	Netherlands	Amsterdam/The Hague	41 526	16 665 000	401	11	81	83	0.5
	New Zealand	Wellington	270 534	4 415 000	16	15	81	86	0.9
	Nicaragua	Managua	130 000	5 870 000	45	24	74	58	1.4
	Niger	Niamey	1 267 000	16 069 000	13	49	54	18	3.5
	Nigeria	Abuja	923 768	162 471 000	176	40	51	50	2.5
	North Korea	P'yŏngyang	120 538	24 451 000	203	14	69	60	0.4
	Norway	Oslo	323 878	4 925 000	15	13	81	79	1.3
	Oman	Muscat	309 500	2 846 000	9	18	73	73	2.3
	Pakistan	Islamabad	803 940	176 745 000	220	27	65	36	1.8
	Palau	Melekeok	497	21 000	42	..	..	84	0.7
	Panama	Panama City	77 082	3 571 000	46	20	76	75	1.5
	Papua New Guinea	Port Moresby	462 840	7 014 000	15	30	62	13	2.2
	Paraguay	Asunción	406 752	6 568 000	16	24	72	62	1.7
	Peru	Lima	1 285 216	29 400 000	23	20	74	77	1.1
	Philippines	Manila	300 000	94 852 000	316	25	68	49	1.7
	Poland	Warsaw	312 683	38 299 000	122	11	76	61	0.1
	Portugal	Lisbon	88 940	10 690 000	120	10	79	61	0.0
	Qatar	Doha	11 437	1 870 000	164	13	78	99	6.1
	Romania	Bucharest	237 500	21 436 000	90	10	73	53	-0.2
	Russian Federation	Moscow	17 075 400	142 836 000	8	13	69	74	0.0
	Rwanda	Kigali	26 338	10 943 000	415	41	55	19	3.0
	St Kitts & Nevis	Basseterre	261	53 000	203	..	..	32	1.2

.. no data availa

Flag	Country	Capital city	Area sq km	Total population 2011	Density persons per sq km 2011	Birth rate per 1000 population 2010	Life expectancy in years 2010	Urban population % 2011	Population change annual % 2011
	St Lucia	Castries	616	176 000	286	13	74	18	1.1
	St Vincent & the Grenadines	Kingstown	389	109 000	280	17	72	49	0.0
	Samoa	Apia	2 831	184 000	65	25	72	20	0.4
	São Tomé & Príncipe	São Tomé	964	169 000	175	31	64	63	1.9
	Saudi Arabia	Riyadh	2 200 000	28 083 000	13	22	74	82	2.3
	Senegal	Dakar	196 720	12 768 000	65	37	59	43	2.6
	Serbia	Belgrade	77 453	7 306 677	94	9	74	56	-0.4
	Seychelles	Victoria	455	87 000	191	18	73	54	-0.6
	Sierra Leone	Freetown	71 740	5 997 000	84	39	47	39	2.2
	Singapore	Singapore	639	5 188 000	8119	9	82	100	2.1
	Slovakia	Bratislava	49 035	5 472 000	112	11	75	55	0.2
	Slovenia	Ljubljana	20 251	2 035 000	100	11	79	50	0.2
	Solomon Islands	Honiara	28 370	552 000	19	32	67	20	2.6
	Somalia	Mogadishu	637 657	9 557 000	15	44	51	38	2.4
	South Africa, Republic of	Pretoria/Cape Town	1 219 090	50 460 000	41	21	52	62	1.2
	South Korea	Seoul	99 274	48 391 000	487	9	81	83	0.7
	South Sudan	Juba	644 329	8 260 490	13	..	..	18	3.6
	Spain	Madrid	504 782	46 455 000	92	11	82	77	0.4
	Sri Lanka	Sri Jayewardenepura Kotte	65 610	21 045 000	321	18	75	15	1.0
	Sudan	Khartoum	1 861 484	36 371 510	20	33	61	33	2.1
	Suriname	Paramaribo	163 820	529 000	3	18	70	70	0.9
	Swaziland	Mbabane	17 364	1 203 000	69	29	48	21	1.2
	Sweden	Stockholm	449 964	9 441 000	21	12	81	85	0.8
	Switzerland	Bern	41 293	7 702 000	187	10	82	74	1.0
	Syria	Damascus	185 180	20 766 000	112	23	76	56	1.8
	Taiwan	T'aipei	36 179	23 164 000	640	..	..	..	..
	Tajikistan	Dushanbe	143 100	6 977 000	49	28	67	27	1.4
	Tanzania	Dodoma	945 087	46 218 000	49	41	57	27	3.0
	Thailand	Bangkok	513 115	69 519 000	135	12	74	34	0.6
	Togo	Lomé	56 785	6 155 000	108	32	57	38	2.1
	Tonga	Nuku'alofa	748	105 000	140	27	72	23	0.4
	Trinidad & Tobago	Port of Spain	5 130	1 346 000	262	15	70	14	0.4
	Tunisia	Tunis	164 150	10 594 000	65	18	75	66	1.0
	Turkey	Ankara	779 452	73 640 000	94	18	74	71	1.2
	Turkmenistan	Ashgabat	488 100	5 105 000	10	22	65	49	1.2
	Uganda	Kampala	241 038	34 509 000	143	45	54	16	3.2
	Ukraine	Kiev	603 700	45 190 000	75	11	70	69	-0.4
	United Arab Emirates	Abu Dhabi	77 700	7 891 000	102	13	77	84	4.9
	United Kingdom	London	243 609	62 417 000	256	13	80	80	0.7
	United States of America	Washington	9 826 635	313 085 000	32	14	78	82	0.7
	Uruguay	Montevideo	176 215	3 380 000	19	14	76	93	0.4
	Uzbekistan	Tashkent	447 400	27 760 000	62	23	68	36	2.7
	Vanuatu	Port Vila	12 190	246 000	20	30	71	25	2.5
	Venezuela	Caracas	912 050	29 437 000	32	21	74	94	1.5
	Vietnam	Ha Nôi	329 565	88 792 000	269	17	75	31	1.0
	Yemen	San'ā'	527 968	24 800 000	47	38	65	32	3.1
	Zambia	Lusaka	752 614	13 475 000	18	46	48	39	4.2
	Zimbabwe	Harare	390 759	12 754 000	33	29	50	39	1.4

.. no data available

The important names on the reference maps in the atlas are found in the index. The names are listed in alphabetical order. Each entry gives the country or region of the world in which the name is located followed by the page number, its alphanumeric grid reference and then its co-ordinates of latitude and longitude. Names of very large areas may have these co-ordinates omitted. Area names which are included in the index are referenced to the centre of the feature. In the case of rivers, the mouth or confluence is taken as the point of reference. It is therefore necessary to follow the river upstream from this point to find its name on the map.

On the map of part of Ireland to the right Dublin is found in grid square E3 at latitude 53° 21'N longitude 6° 18'W.

This appears in the index as   **Dublin** Ireland **25 E3** 53.21N 6.18W .
The chart below explains all the elements listed for each entry.

Dublin	Ireland	25	E3	53.21N	6.18W
Name of the feature to be located.	Name of the country in which the feature is situated.	Page in the atlas where the feature is shown on the largest scale.	Grid square where the feature is found.	Degrees and minutes north or south of the equator.	Degrees and minutes east or west of Greenwich meridian.

Sometimes an abbreviated description of a feature is included in the entry. A list of abbreviations used in the index is included below.

Abbreviations

Afghan.	Afghanistan	Dem. Rep.	Democratic Republic of	**Mt.**	Mount	*resr.*	reservoir
Austa.	Australasia	Congo	the Congo	*mtn.*	mountain	R.S.A.	Republic of South Africa
b., **B.**	bay, Bay	Equat. Guinea	Equatorial Guinea	*mts.*, **Mts.**	mountains	Russian Fed.	Russian Federation
Bangla.	Bangladesh	*est.*	estuary	N. America	North America	Serb.	Serbia
Bosnia.	Bosnia-Herzegovina	*f.*	physical feature eg. valley,	Neth.	Netherlands	S. America	South America
c., **C.**	cape, Cape		plain	N. Korea	North Korea	S. Korea	South Korea
C. America	Central America	**G.**	Gulf	**Oc.**	Ocean	*str.*, **Str.**	strait, Strait
C.A.R.	Central African Republic	I.o.M	Isle of Man	*pen.*, **Pen.**	peninsula, Peninsula	Switz.	Switzerland
d.	Internal division eg. state,	*l.* **L.**	lake, Lake	Phil.	Philippines	U.K.	United Kingdom
	county	Lux.	Luxembourg	P.N.G.	Papua New Guinea	U.S.A.	United States of America
des.	desert	Mont.	Montenegro	*r.*	river	W. Sahara	Western Sahara

A

Aberdeen Scotland **24 F4** 57.08N 2.07W
Aberystwyth Wales **23 C4** 52.25N 4.06W
Abidjan Côte d'Ivoire **50 C5** 5.19N 4.01W
Abu Dhabi U.A.E. **38 E3** 24.27N 54.23E
Abuja Nigeria **50 D5** 9.12N 7.11E
Acapulco Mexico **59 J4** 16.51N 99.56W
Accra Ghana **50 C5** 5.33N 0.15W
Aconcagua, Cerro *mtn.* Argentina **63 D3** 32.37S 70.00W
Adamawa Highlands Nigeria/Cameroon **50 E5** 7.05N 12.00E
Adana Turkey **31 G2** 37.00N 35.19E
Addis Ababa Ethiopia **50 G5** 9.03N 38.42E
Adelaide Australia **70 D2** 34.56S 138.36E
Aden, G. of Indian Oc. **38 D2** 13.00N 50.00E
Adriatic Sea Med. Sea **32 F5** 42.30N 16.00E
Aegean Sea Med. Sea **30 F2** 39.00N 25.00E
Afghanistan Asia **38 F4** 33.00N 65.30E
Africa 48–50
Ahmadabad India **39 G3** 23.03N 72.40E
Albania Europe **30 E3** 41.00N 20.00E
Aleppo Syria **38 C4** 36.14N 37.10E
Alexandria Egypt **50 F8** 31.13N 29.55E
Algeria Africa **50 C7** 28.00N 2.00E
Algiers Algeria **50 D8** 36.50N 3.00E
Alice Springs Australia **70 D3** 23.42S 133.52E
Allier *r.* France **30 D4** 46.58N 3.04E
Alps *mts.* Europe **30 D3** 46.00N 7.30E
Altai Mts. Mongolia **40 B8** 46.30N 93.30E
Altiplano *f.* Bolivia **64 C4** 18.00S 67.30W
Amazon *r.* Brazil **64 F7** 2.00S 50.00W
Amazon, Mouths of the *f.* Brazil **64 G8** 0.00 50.00W
'Ammān Jordan **38 C4** 31.57N 35.56E
Amsterdam Neth. **30 D4** 52.22N 4.54E
Amur *r.* Russian Fed. **36 J6** 53.17N 140.00E
Anápolis Brazil **64 G4** 16.19S 48.58W
Anchorage U.S.A. **58 E9** 61.10N 150.00W
Andaman Is. India **39 I2** 12.00N 93.00E
Andaman Sea Indian Oc. **39 I2** 11.00N 96.00E
Andes *mts.* S. America **62 D5** 15.00S 74.00W
Andorra Europe **30 D3** 42.30N 1.32E
Angola Africa **51 E3** 12.00S 18.00E
Ankara Turkey **31 G2** 39.55N 32.50E
Anshan China **40 E8** 41.05N 122.58E
Antananarivo Madagascar **51 H3** 18.52S 47.30E

Antarctica 75
Antigua and Barbuda Lesser Antilles **62 E8** 17.30N 61.49W
Antofagasta Chile **63 D4** 23.40S 70.23W
Aoraki *mtn.* New Zealand **71 H1** 43.36S 170.09E
Apennines *mts.* Italy **32 D6** 44.00N 11.00E
Appalachian Mts. U.S.A. **59 K6** 39.30N 78.00W
Arabian Sea Asia **38 F2** 19.00N 65.00E
Arafura Sea Austa. **70 D5** 9.00S 135.00E
Araguaína Brazil **64 G6** 7.16S 48.18W
Araguari Brazil **64 G4** 18.38S 48.13W
Aral Sea Asia **38 E5** 45.00N 60.00E
Archangel Russian Fed. **31 H5** 64.32N 41.10E
Arctic Ocean 74
Arequipa Peru **64 B4** 16.25S 71.32W
Argentina S. America **63 E3** 35.00S 65.00W
Arica Chile **62 D5** 18.30S 70.20W
Arkansas *r.* U.S.A. **59 J6** 33.50N 91.00W
Armenia Asia **38 D5** 40.00N 45.00E
Arnhem Land *f.* Australia **70 D4** 13.00S 132.30E
Aruba *i.* Lesser Antilles **62 D8** 12.30N 70.00W
Arusha Tanzania **52 C4** 3.21S 36.40E
Ashford England **23 H3** 51.08N 0.53E
Asia 36–37
Asmara Eritrea **50 G6** 15.20N 38.58E
Asunción Paraguay **63 F4** 25.15S 57.40W
Atacama Desert S. America **63 D4** 20.00S 69.00W
Athens Greece **30 F2** 37.59N 23.42E
Atlanta U.S.A. **59 K4** 33.45N 84.23W
Atlantic Ocean 76 G7
Atlas Mts. Africa **50 C8** 33.00N 4.00W
Auckland New Zealand **71 H2** 36.52S 174.45E
Australia Austa. **70** 25.00S 135.00E
Austria Europe **30 E3** 47.30N 14.00E
Ayers Rock *see* **Uluru** Australia **70**
Ayr Scotland **24 D2** 55.28N 4.37W
Azerbaijan Asia **38 D5** 40.10N 47.50E
Azov, Sea of Ukraine **31 G3** 46.00N 36.30E

B

Baffin B. Canada **58 M10** 74.00N 70.00W
Baffin I. Canada **58 L9** 68.50N 70.00W
Baghdād Iraq **38 D4** 33.20N 44.26E
Bahrain Asia **38 E3** 26.00N 50.35E
Baikal, L. Russian Fed. **40 C9** 53.30N 108.00E
Baja California *pen.* Mexico **59 H5** 27.00N 113.00W
Baku Azerbaijan **38 D5** 40.22N 49.53E

Balbina, Represa de *resr.* Brazil **64 E7** 1.30S 60.00W
Balearic Is. Spain **30 D2** 39.30N 2.30E
Balkan Mts. Bulgaria **30 F3** 42.50N 24.30E
Balkhash, L. Kazakhstan **36 F6** 46.51N 75.00E
Baltic Sea Europe **30 E4** 56.30N 19.00E
Baltimore U.S.A. **58 L6** 39.18N 76.38W
Bamako Mali **50 C6** 12.40N 7.59W
Bandar Seri Begawan Brunei **41 D4** 4.56N 114.58E
Bangalore India **39 G2** 12.58N 77.35E
Bangkok Thailand **41 C5** 13.45N 100.35E
Bangladesh Asia **39 H3** 24.00N 90.00E
Bangui C.A.R. **50 E5** 4.23N 18.37E
Baotou China **40 D8** 40.38N 109.59E
Barbados Lesser Antilles **62 F8** 13.20N 59.40W
Barcelona Spain **30 D3** 41.25N 2.10E
Barents Sea Arctic Oc. **36 D7** 73.00N 40.00E
Barquisimeto Venezuela **62 E8** 10.03N 69.18W
Barranquilla Colombia **62 D8** 11.00N 74.50W
Basel Switz. **30 D3** 47.33N 7.36E
Bass Str. Australia **70 E2** 39.45S 146.00E
Bath England **23 E3** 51.22N 2.22W
Beijing China **40 D7** 39.55N 116.25E
Beirut Lebanon **38 C4** 33.52N 35.30E
Belarus Europe **30 F4** 53.00N 28.00E
Belém Brazil **64 G7** 1.27S 48.29W
Belfast N. Ireland **24 F4** 54.36N 5.57W
Belgium Europe **30 D4** 51.00N 4.30E
Belgrade Serb. **30 F3** 44.49N 20.28E
Belize C. America **59 K4** 17.00N 88.30W
Belmopan Belize **59 K4** 17.25N 88.46W
Belo Horizonte Brazil **65 H4** 19.45S 43.53W
Ben Nevis *mtn.* Scotland **24 D3** 56.48N 5.00W
Bengal, B. of Indian Oc. **39 H2** 17.00N 89.00E
Benin Africa **50 D5** 9.00N 2.30E
Benin, Bight of *b.* Africa **50 D5** 5.30N 3.00E
Bergen Norway **30 D5** 60.23N 5.20E
Bering Sea N. America/Asia **37 N6** 60.00N 170.00W
Berlin Germany **30 E4** 52.32N 13.25E
Bermuda *i.* Atlantic Oc. **59 M6** 32.18N 65.00W
Bern Switz. **30 D3** 46.57N 7.26E
Berwick-upon-Tweed England **22 E7** 55.46N 2.00W
Bhutan Asia **39 I3** 27.25N 90.00E
Bié Plateau *f.* Angola **51 E3** 13.00S 16.00E
Birmingham England **23 F4** 52.30N 1.55W
Biscay, B. of France **30 C3** 45.30N 3.00W
Bissau Guinea-Bissau **50 B6** 11.52N 15.39W
Black Sea Europe **31 G3** 43.00N 35.00E

Blackburn England **22 E5** 53.44N 2.30W
Blackpool England **22 D5** 53.48N 3.03W
Blanc, Mont *mtn.* Europe **30 D3** 45.50N 6.52E
Bogotá Colombia **62 D7** 4.38N 74.05W
Bolivia S. America **62 E5** 17.00S 65.00W
Bologna Italy **32 D6** 44.30N 11.20E
Bolton England **22 E5** 53.35N 2.26W
Bombay *see* **Mumbai** India **39**
Bonn Germany **30 D4** 50.44N 7.06E
Bordeaux France **30 C3** 44.50N 0.34W
Borneo *i.* Asia **41 D4** 1.00N 114.00E
Bosnia-Herzegovina Europe **30 E3** 44.00N 18.00E
Boston U.S.A. **58 L7** 42.15N 71.05W
Bothnia, G. of Europe **30 E5** 63.30N 20.30E
Botswana Africa **51 F2** 22.00S 24.00E
Bournemouth England **23 F2** 50.43N 1.53W
Bradford England **22 F5** 53.47N 1.45W
Brasília Brazil **64 G4** 15.54S 47.50W
Bratislava Slovakia **30 E3** 48.10N 17.10E
Brazil S. America **64–65** 10.00S 52.00W
Brazilian Highlands Brazil **64 G5** 17.00S 48.00W
Brazzaville Congo **50 E4** 4.14S 15.14E
Brighton England **23 G2** 50.50N 0.09W
Brisbane Australia **70 F3** 27.30S 153.00E
Bristol England **23 E3** 51.26N 2.35W
Bristol Channel England/Wales **23 C3** 51.17N 3.20W
British Isles Europe **26 D5** 54.00N 5.00W
Brunei Asia **41 D4** 4.56N 114.58E
Brussels Belgium **30 D4** 50.50N 4.23E
Bucharest Romania **30 F3** 44.25N 26.06E
Budapest Hungary **30 E3** 47.30N 19.03E
Buenos Aires Argentina **63 F3** 34.40S 58.30W
Bujumbura Burundi **52 A4** 3.22S 29.21E
Bulgaria Europe **30 F3** 42.30N 25.00E
Burkina Faso Africa **50 C6** 12.15N 1.30W
Burma *see* **Myanmar** Asia **39**
Bursa Turkey **30 F3** 40.11N 29.04E
Burundi Africa **52 A4** 3.30S 30.00E

C

Caernarfon Wales **22 C5** 53.08N 4.17W
Cagliari Italy **32 C3** 39.14N 9.07E
Cairns Australia **70 E4** 16.51S 145.43E
Cairo Egypt **50 G8** 30.03N 31.15E
Calais France **30 D4** 50.57N 1.50E
Calcutta *see* **Kolkata** India **39**
Calgary Canada **58 H8** 51.05N 114.05W